The
Secret
of the
Stairs

The
Secret
of the
Stairs

by

Wade E. Taylor

McDougal Publishing is a ministry of The McDougal Foundation, Inc., a Maryland nonprofit corporation dedicated to spreading the Gospel of the Lord Jesus Christ to as many people as possible in the shortest time possible.

Third Edition
First Printing – October 1993
Second Printing – December 1994
Third Printing – August 1996
Fourth Printing – May 1998
Fifth Printing – July 2001
Sixth Printing – August 2003

Published by:

McDougal Publishing
P.O. Box 3595
Hagerstown, MD 21742-3595
www.mcdougalpublishing.com

ISBN 1-884369-35-9

Printed in the United States of America
For Worldwide Distribution

Contents

Introduction

The message of the Song of Solomon is directed toward those who are already saved and have an understanding, to some measure, of Romans 6:11.

"Likewise reckon ye also yourselves to be dead indeed unto sin, but alive unto God through Jesus Christ our Lord."

Also, having the infilling of the Holy Spirit will be an immeasurable help in being able to understand and experientially receive the message and purpose of this book.

The Song of Solomon sets forth the development of a beautiful love-relationship between our Heavenly Bridegroom and His Bride in such expressive imagery that we are enlightened, challenged, and drawn closer to Him. It not only reveals the desire of the Lord to draw us into quality times of intimate communion and ministry with Him, it also presents the method and means by which this can be accomplished.

This applies to those who have fully consecrated their lives to the Lord and have "touched" Him in some measure, yet still have a burning hunger to better know Him, and to grow spiritually.

We may have a wonderful testimony: "The Lord told me to go . . . or the Lord said to do . . ." but there is something beyond this which the Lord greatly desires. This was shown to me in a very special way when the Lord had quickened to me a country in South America.

As I prayerfully held this before the Lord, I felt I had completely consecrated my life on this point. I was willing to go, and waited only for the Lord's confirmation.

I said, "Lord, why don't You speak and tell me; then I will know what to do?" A short time later, the Lord unfolded the following understanding to me through a very clear impression within my spirit: "If I speak and tell you to go, it will destroy the very thing that I desire to accomplish within your life. If I were to continually speak to you and say 'go' here or there; or 'do' this or that, our relationship would become like that of an employer and employee. When an employer tells his employee, 'I want you to do thus and so,' the employee responds, 'Yes, sir, I will do it.' Then, at the end of the week, after he has done all these things, he returns to his employer with his hand out, saying, 'I have done all you required of me, now I am ready for my paycheck.'"

After I saw this, the Lord clearly said: "I desire our relationship to be as an intimate love-relationship; that of a bridegroom with his bride, rather than that of an employer and employee." He is our head, we are the members of His body. Therefore, we are to flow together with Him as one. Jesus prayed for this oneness in our relationship to Him.

> "That they all may be one; as Thou, Father, art in Me, and I in Thee, that they also may be one in Us: that the world may believe that Thou hast sent Me" John 17:21.

We are to become one with Him, in intent and in experience even as Jesus exhibited, or manifested, the Father on earth. Jesus said, "He that hath seen Me hath seen the Father" John 14:9b. He was saying, "I so perfectly do the will of My Father and am so completely in accord with Him, that all I say or do is exactly as He would have said or done and reflects Him. Therefore, if you have seen Me, you have seen Him."

Jesus said, "Ye shall be witnesses" Acts 1:8b. This means that I am to come into such intimate unity with my Lord that my life will reflect, or set forth, His nature and character. My life should witness to, or reveal Him in such completion and fullness that I could say as Paul, "If you have seen me, you have seen Jesus." This is what the Lord meant when He said to me, "I do not want our relationship to be that of an employer and employee. Instead, it is to be as a marriage relationship in which there is such a oneness and unity that I will be able to reveal Myself through you."

Paul said in Galatians 2:20a, "I am crucified with Christ." This word "crucified" expresses the fact that the "I" has been put to death. In the beginning there was only one will, the will of God. All creation was submitted to His will, and resounded to the Glory of God in obedience and harmony. Then, Lucifer rose up and said, "I will ascend . . . I will be like the most High" Is 14:13b, 14b. Now, there were two wills, "Thy will" and "I will."

These two wills were contrary, the one to the other, forming a cross in heaven before there ever was one on earth. Then Lucifer caused sin to enter the Garden of Eden. Now these two conflicting wills adversely affected the earth and the man that God had created. Jesus came and died on this cross, paying the full penalty for the resultant sin, and made it possible for us to again choose "Thy will" and then function with Him in obedience and harmony. Jesus said,

> "If any man will come after Me, let him deny himself, and take up his cross, and follow Me" Matt 16:24b.

To take up my cross means that I must cross-out my "self-will," or my "I-will." This crucifies my own will (ways) and I again become one-with-Him. Thus, my will is submitted to and merged into His will. Now, His will has become my will and I am free to follow Him.

When the Scripture says that "we crucify Christ afresh," it means that "my will" again rises up against the will of God (Heb 6:6). I press to have my own way, grieving and breaking the heart of the Lord. As He chastens me in love, I respond by quickly bringing my own desires to the cross, for I have learned that His will for me is far better than anything I may desire. He died that we might become one with Him. He gave His Spirit to abide within us that we might come forth into the victory and fullness of His Body completed—our being in perfect union and communion with Him.

The Lord desires to bring us into the place where our will is merged into His will, where we are no longer working **for** Him, but are joined together to Him, becoming one with Him, as in a marriage.

"Who is this that cometh up from the wilderness, **leaning** upon her Beloved?" SS 8:5a.

The desire of the Lord, as revealed in the Song of Solomon, is to make known to us the "way" of entrance to the stairs that lead upward into His chambers. As we partake of the message within this book, The Secret of the Stairs, we will progress ever upward upon these stairs, that we might come into this experience of union and communion with Him.

The Lord seeks a Bride who is willing to yield her life and her identity that she might come into a life of complete submission to, and union with, her Heavenly Bridegroom.

"My Beloved spake, and said unto me, Rise up, My love, My fair one, and come away" SS 2:10.

This speaks of the exquisite joy of being one with Him. Let us begin this journey into His chambers. There, we will find the satisfaction for which we were created.

Preface

The Song of Solomon reveals the processes of God, which unfold within the lives of those who are seeking to know Him more fully and personally.

The principles that are revealed within this book will guide us from our new birth through to spiritual maturity. As we personally respond to His desire for a Bride, this book will become a priceless guide that will lead us to the Bridegroom within His chambers.

The spiritual truths which are hidden within the Song of Solomon can be extracted and understood only through a developing love-relationship with the Lord Himself. Those who approach this book intellectually will never be able to plumb the depths of the truths it contains.

The King James Version has been followed throughout The Secret of the Stairs as it more closely expresses the divine intention in the Song of Solomon. Any exception is noted with the reference. Most translations depict a human love affair rather than that of a Heavenly Bridegroom seeking out a Bride from among the Daughters, His Church.

"I love them that love Me; and those that seek Me early shall find Me . . . that I may cause those that love Me to inherit substance; and I will fill their treasures" Prov 8:17, 21.

As we seek to better know the Lord, we must learn to listen to Him in our spirit, rather than through our mind. There is a spiritual "listening" which can be cultivated within those who are redeemed. Jesus said,

"Who hath ears to hear, let him hear" Matt 13:9.

He is not speaking about our physical ability to hear. We are in essence a spiritual being, and within us is an inner ear, the ear of our spirit, through which we hear spiritually.

As we listen to Him with this inner spiritual ear, truth is deposited in our spirit. It may take months, or even years, for the Lord to organize the circumstances of our lives in such a way that this truth may be released, to move from the innermost depths of our being, up into our consciousness.

We tend to reverse this process by approaching truth with our intellect and then try to force spiritual facts and information into our minds, thinking that all this will simultaneously be received into our spirit.

Truth always moves upward. Therefore, when anointed, truth is imparted within our spirits, and then progressively works its way up from our spirit into the realm of our understanding. As we patiently hold our spirits before the Lord, this process of spiritual transfer, or osmosis, takes place. This results in the Lord being able to more fully reveal Himself to us and to satisfy our spiritual hunger and desire for Him.

To better receive the rich deposit of spiritual truth that is hidden within its pages, we should, with heart-sincerity, give expression to this prayer as we begin to read the Song of Solomon along with its companion, <u>The Secret of the Stairs</u>.

Lord, I ask You to enlarge my spiritual hunger and capacity. Anoint and guide me as I begin to partake of the Song of Solomon. Release me from every hindrance, that I might begin to move into the spiritual reality that You have waiting for me within its pages.

I love You, Lord, and I trust You with my life. Without qualification, I totally place myself in Your hands that You might work the message of this book into the fiber of my being. Create within me the capacity to understand the spiritual principles contained in this book.

Lord, I ask that these truths become personalized within me. Only then will I be changed, and others helped through my experience.

Only You can make of me the Bride that You desire, as You have revealed throughout the Song of Solomon. I ask that You move in my life to cause me to become this Bride that You so longingly desire.

I thank You, Lord Jesus. Amen.

Chapter 1

Draw Me

"The song of songs,
which is Solomon's"
SS 1:1.

The message within the Song of Solomon develops around a Bridegroom Who actively seeks a Bride from among the Daughters of Jerusalem. In order to understand the message of this book and then receive from it the value it has for us, we must prayerfully read ourselves into the progressive action that unfolds within its pages.

This Bridegroom is our Lord Jesus Christ. He is **still** seeking after and preparing a Bride from those within the Church of our day who will respond to Him. The Song of Solomon is invaluable to those who desire to have a part in the coming "marriage supper of the Lamb."

> "And he saith unto me, Write, **Blessed are they which are called** unto the marriage supper of the Lamb. And he saith unto me, These are the true sayings of God" Rev 19:9.

The Lord greatly desires that we choose Him above all else, that we may become a part of this corporate **Bride** that He is yet apprehending and preparing. As we progressively respond to Him, He will determinedly draw us, step upon step, ever upward toward His chambers. Here, we become one as we partake with

15

Him in intimate fellowship and participate with Him in the outworking of His purposes.

The Daughters of Jerusalem depict the many Christians who view and relate to the Bridegroom in a different (lesser) realm than His Bride, with whom He desires to be fully united. Although these Daughters will not be called to the coming "marriage supper of the Lamb," they continually affect the developing relationship between the Bride and the Bridegroom.

As we prayerfully compare our desires and goals with those of the Daughters of Jerusalem, we will gain much understanding concerning our spiritual condition and the corrections that should be made. Also, we will be challenged, as was the Apostle Paul, to "press toward the mark for the prize of the high calling of God in Christ Jesus" Phil 3:14; for there is far more available to us than just maintaining our salvation.

We will benefit most from the Song of Solomon by comparing our attitudes and responses to the Lord with those of the Bride to the Bridegroom. As the hindrances to her relationship with the Bridegroom unfold before us, we should begin to recognize similar problems within our spiritual lives. Then we will be able to make the changes she makes in order to become one with Him. We must qualify and be chosen by Him to become His Bride.

> "For many are called, but few are chosen"
> Matt 22:14.

All this begins with the expression of her heart's desire toward the Bridegroom,

> "Draw me, we will run after Thee . . ."

and the result,

> "The King hath brought me into His chambers"
> SS 1:4.

16

This prayer of desire, and the declaration of her willingness to respond to any steps that He might take toward her, turned the heart of the Bridegroom and set the stage for all that follows in the development of their relationship as seen throughout the Song of Solomon.

The first part is an extremely important prayer, consisting of only two words: "Draw me." Next, she makes a firm commitment to the Bridegroom: "We will run after Thee." The third part is the glorious result of her desire and consecration: "The King hath brought me into His chambers."

This essential prayer, "Draw me," relates to our spiritual hunger. Hunger is basic to all life and finds its satisfaction in many forms. Our spiritual hunger is a part of this. It must overcome and rise above all of the natural "urges of life" that are deep within us and motivate our actions in relation to our self-life. As we lift our desire for the Lord above all other desires, and determine that He, and He alone, will feed and satisfy this hunger, we are truly ready to be brought into His chambers.

We must come to this experience of intense spiritual hunger and desire for the Lord. In the physical realm, a baby is born hungry. The mother does not create the child's natural hunger; she simply satisfies it. Spiritual hunger cannot be created by man. It is the result of a creative act of God and comes only from Him. This is why the Bride cried out, "Draw me." At the beginning of their relationship, she wanted her desire for Him to be enlarged.

We must "wait upon" or quietly hold ourselves before the Lord, so this spiritual hunger may be created within us. As this hunger begins to manifest itself, and we cry out for its satisfaction, the Lord will come in anticipation of making Himself known to us.

> "Behold, I stand at the door, and knock: if any man hear My voice, and open the door, I will come in to him, and will sup with him, and he with Me" Rev 3:20.

Only as we enter into this relationship of intimately knowing Him will we find the completion that was intended in our original creation. Then, the outworking of our growth into the fully developed Bride that He desires will begin.

> "Let us rejoice and be exceeding glad, and let us give the glory unto Him: for the marriage of the Lamb is come, and **His wife hath made herself ready**. And it was given unto her that she should array herself in fine linen, bright and pure: for the fine linen is the righteous acts of the saints" Rev 19:7-8 ASV.

Thus, spiritual hunger is the foundation of our spiritual life. We must be careful to separate this spiritual "emptiness" that desires satisfaction from all other desires or things, and not allow some substitute to seemingly satisfy it. Nor should we seek some other means than the Lord Himself to "feed" our spiritual hunger.

The next step begins with her declaration: "We will run after Thee." The word "we" portrays every part of our being totally seeking after and responding to the Lord. Paul said, "I am crucified with Christ: nevertheless I live; yet not I, but Christ liveth in me" Gal 2:20a. We may quote this verse and even testify about it. But there is a spiritual law involved. Truth is never ours until we have experienced it and it has become a part of us. Then we too can say, "I live; yet not I."

We must be certain that we have "counted the cost" and are fully determined to "run after Him" because the Lord will respond to this commitment. He will begin by causing the "letter" of His Word that is within us to become "experientially" a part of us. As a result, our understanding of the Word and of our spiritual experiences will become so alive and real within us that we will see Jesus at the center of them, and begin to experientially know and love Him as never before.

He will arrange all of the necessary circumstances to make this possible. We must be careful to recognize the spiritual purpose and value in the things we experience in our daily pattern of life. There are no "accidents" in the life of one who has made this commitment.

The Scripture says concerning Jesus,

> "The Word was made flesh, and dwelt among us" John 1:14a.

The Word of God is never mine until it has been personalized in my life experience. Only then can I, with authority, witness to its truth and power. As Jesus was baptized by John and came up out of the water, the heavens opened and the Spirit of God descended as a dove, settling upon Him. Then the Father spoke, "This is My beloved Son, in Whom I am well pleased" Matt 3:17b. This was a tremendous blessing, but there was something more for Jesus to experience before this Word that He received from His Father could become "flesh" and "power" within His life.

Jesus came up out of the water **full of the Holy Spirit** (Luke 4:1). He had received the blessing and impartation. Now, the Word that had been spoken over Him had to become personalized, or made "flesh" within His life experience. The next thing the Scripture says is that **He was driven**. He was compelled by the Holy Spirit to go into the wilderness (Mark 1:12). There, He was tested for 40 days—"40" being the number of testing. By the end of this time, Jesus had overcome every temptation, and had defeated Satan. Then Jesus came forth from the wilderness in the POWER of the Spirit (Luke 4:14).

The fullness had become power because truth had been personalized in His life through experience.

> "For we are His workmanship, created in Christ Jesus unto good works, which God hath before ordained that we should walk in them" Eph 2:10.

We are the "product" that He is producing. He is working in our lives with the specific goal of making us conformable to the image and likeness of His Son, the Lord Jesus Christ.

> "For whom He did foreknow, He also did predestinate to be conformed to the image of His Son" Rom 8:29a.

In our day, the Lord is bringing forth a people who are willing to be tested and proven in order to become all He has determined them to be, that they might be able to buy of Him "gold tried in the fire" Rev 3:18a. He is searching for those who are not spiritually lazy, or content to rest in the blessings and gifts of the Spirit, which they have freely received.

There are those who are willing to go into the wilderness and face intense hunger until they are fed by the Lord Himself. Afterwards, these will come forth victorious in the power of the Spirit to rise into this higher realm of identity with Him.

Acts 1:8a tells us, "But ye shall receive power, AFTER." Power in our Christian experience does not come as a result of our receiving the fullness of the Spirit. There is something more required for His power to come into our lives. Jesus received the fullness of the Spirit in the Jordan, but he went into the wilderness for a time of testing and proving (Luke 4:1-14). Here, "the Word became flesh"—it became power in His life. Now, when Jesus ministered, men became attentive and said, "Never man spake like this Man" John 7:46. Why? Because the Word and the flesh (His life experience in proven submission to His Father) were one. This is the "oneness" which the Lord desires to work into our lives.

If we sincerely pray "Draw me," and make this unconditional commitment to the Lord "We will run after Thee," the Lord will accept our prayer and begin His work within us. We will be given the Baptism in the Holy Spirit, the gifts and the blessings that follow, and all of the "divine arrangements" that are necessary to accomplish our time of wilderness testing. As we faithfully pass through these, His presence within us and His Word to us will become more than just a blessing or a testimony that we share. It will become spiritual power that has been personalized within our lives, bringing us into a unity of purpose and oneness with the Lord.

"And they were astonished at His doctrine: for His Word was with power" Luke 4:32.

"We will run after Thee." "Lord, in the totality of my being: my spirit, my soul, and my body; my will, my intellect, and my emotions; all that I ever was, all that I am now, and all that I ever will be; Lord, WE—all of me—will respond to Your hand upon, and Your activity within my life. The Word You quickened within me, the revelation You have shown me, all that You have given to me must be incorporated into my life experience so I will be in harmony and in union with You. Lord, in submission and in devotion, I will respond to You and cooperate with You as You accomplish all this within my life. And Lord, please do not pay any attention if I complain."

"For many are called, but few are chosen" Matt 22:14.

Another way to say this is: "Many are called, but few are willing to pay the price in order to be chosen." There is a price to pay in coming into the place where His Word has become personalized in our life experience. Then when we speak, we bear witness to this impartation of His Word having become flesh within us. Now, His Word and my life are one, and "we" in this oneness will run after Him.

> "But ye shall receive power, after that the Holy Ghost is come upon you: and ye shall BE witnesses unto Me" Acts 1:8a.

There is a popular saying that the Baptism in the Holy Spirit is "power for service." This is true, but it is far more than that. This power is the "dunamis" *(Greek for dynamo)* of God. It is the enabling power of God that flows through our lives and guides our spiritual development and identification with Him. As a result, we ourselves BECOME this witness.

When Moses went up into the mount, the children of Israel said, "All that the LORD hath said will we do, and be obedient" Ex 24:7b. This was a tremendous intention, but they failed. The Old Testament is written as a testimony that flesh cannot fulfill the law of God. Therefore, the promise of a New Covenant was given.

> "A new heart also will I give you, and a new spirit will I put within you: and I will take away the stony heart out of your flesh, and I will give you an heart of flesh. And I will put My Spirit within you, and cause you to walk in My statutes, and ye shall keep My judgments, and do them" Ezek 36:26-27.

The Baptism in the Holy Spirit is given as part of the fulfillment of this prophetic promise in Ezekiel.

> "But ye shall receive **power**, after that the Holy Ghost is come upon you: and ye shall be witnesses unto Me" Acts 1:8a.

It is the power of the Holy Spirit that causes, or enables us to walk, and to continue walking in His statutes. This "power" in Acts 1:8 is the same as the "cause" in Ezekiel 36:27. These are one and the same in their purpose and effect.

Thus, the Baptism in the Holy Spirit is far more than "power for service." Christian service is something that I **"do"** for the Lord. However, this verse does not say anything about doing; rather, it tells me that I am to **"be"** a witness. "Being" speaks of what I am, rather than what I do. My "witness" is the expression of what I have "become" in Him. If I am "doing" witnessing, then I am telling someone about the Lord. However, "being" a witness means something far deeper. What I am "seen" to be becomes very important. In being a witness, I am saying or doing exactly what Jesus would say or do if He were here. Therefore, I am a witness, or better, I am a "sample" of Him.

This Baptism will truly enable us to serve Him better, but the real result is that through the power that is imparted into our lives, we personally become witnesses that can be seen as well as heard.

That which I have experienced and become is reflected through my conduct. Now, my life will be a witness of these things. When Philip said, "Shew us the Father," Jesus' reply was, "He that hath seen Me hath seen the Father" John 14:8a, 9b. Jesus was saying, "My life is a witness of the Father to such an extent that if you have seen Me, you have seen the Father."

When the Lord is satisfied that we truly intend to "run after Him," then His processings will begin in our lives. Jesus said, "Ye shall receive power, AFTER." Notice that the "Baptism in the Holy Spirit" is a gift, but the "power" is conditional. It is only available to us, "after." We must go through a time of testing in order to obtain the fullness of this power.

In the Song of Solomon, the work of preparing the Bride begins at the point where most Christians have become satisfied and seek to go no further. The Scripture says, "My people are destroyed for lack of knowledge" Hos 4:6a. In some meetings, the Lord's people are led to make a consecration, and then are left there until the next speaker comes along and leads them to make yet another consecration. This pattern is repeated again and again, with no direction to lead them further.

We asked the Lord to "draw us." Then we consecrated our lives to "run after Him." But this is not the end. There is yet another step that we are to take, "The King hath brought me into His chambers." As we enter this place of intimacy in our personal fellowship with Him, we will receive (as a result of our overcoming victory in being tested and proven) the **enabling power** that will strengthen and guide us through the steps that will prepare us to become His Bride. As we enjoy an increasing degree of communion with Him, we can trust Him to gently lead us through these experiences.

In order to gain the capacity and receive the strength we need during these times of testing, we are drawn into His "chambers" to spend time with Him in the intimacy of His presence alone. Here, as we bask in His presence, we can wait upon Him. This time that we spend "waiting upon the Lord" is of utmost importance.

> "But they that wait upon the LORD shall renew their strength; they shall mount up with wings as eagles; they shall run, and not be weary; and they shall walk, and not faint" Is 40:31.

"The King hath brought me into His chambers." Herein is the secret: we must spend time in communion with our Lord. When we enter His chambers and wait in His presence, the power of God flows into our being. Then we are enabled to minister, or move with

Him in what we have received. We will become weary, but "they that wait upon the LORD shall renew their strength."

It is essential to our spiritual health that we spend time in His presence, waiting upon Him. Only then will we have the spiritual energy to face the challenges, testings, and problems of life.

Our Heavenly Bridegroom brings us into His chambers to abide there with Him. As His Bride, we will experience joy unspeakable, unknown to others. During these times of intimate communion, we are brought into a closer unity with Him. In the closeness of this communion, we will begin to understand spiritual principles and truths that will draw us yet closer. There is no end!

As we pray this little prayer, "Draw me," we are opening the way that will lead us upward, step upon step, into the chambers of heaven. Here, all that we have ever longed for will be found in Him.

"The King hath brought me into His chambers"
SS 1:4b.

Chapter 2

An Overall View

Seeing our Lord as a Heavenly Bridegroom Who is seeking the attention and affection of His Bride will give us a better understanding of the principles that will help us in our desire to better know Him and grow into spiritual maturity.

As we follow the steps that He takes in order to draw His Bride to Himself, we too will be drawn into a closer personal relationship with Him. We will become more responsive to Him when He comes and knocks upon the door of our heart, and more submissive to His dealings within our lives as we identify ourselves with the reluctant and preoccupied Bride who lives within the pages of the Song of Songs.

As we meditate upon the experiences of the Bride in her progress, we should be able to bypass some of the mistakes she made and more readily submit ourselves to the Lord as He draws us into a closer, more intimate relationship to Himself. If we will carefully observe the gradual changes that take place within her, and prayerfully follow her as she moves, step upon step, upward toward His chambers, we will discover the delight of joining her in union and communion with Him.

Also, as we consider the necessary role of the Daughters of Jerusalem in helping, or provoking the Bride to become all that the Bridegroom desires her to be, we will be able to better appreciate our relationship to other Christians. We will recognize that their role is similar to that of the Daughters of Jerusalem in the development of our spiritual lives.

By responding to these things with a right attitude, we can quicken the pace of our spiritual development. If we are not able to do so, the Lord will wait until we are ready. He will never deal with us, or allow others to "affect" us beyond that which we can handle. It is very important that we recognize this.

> "I charge you, O ye Daughters of Jerusalem, by the roes, and by the hinds of the field, that ye stir not up, nor awake My love, till SHE please" SS 2:7 (*"she" NAS margin*).

As we compare our hesitations in responding to our heavenly Bridegroom with those of the Bride, we will realize how far we have strayed from abiding in Him. This will stir us to earnestly pray as she did, "Draw me," and to make the commitment that she made, "We will run after Thee." This most important prayer, asking the Lord to enlarge our spiritual hunger and to establish our consecration to follow Him alone, will release our Heavenly Bridegroom to become active within us and in our circumstances, to change us into the Bride He longingly desires us to become.

No longer will we view the Lord merely as the Supreme Power to Whom we pray in an attempt to cause Him to do as we desire. We will begin to know Him experientially as a "Divine Friend" Who personally loves us, and greatly desires our fellowship. As we look forward to our times of fellowship with Him and begin to respond to His love reaching toward us, we will feel deep within our being a sense of satisfaction and fulfillment.

We were created with this ability to respond to our

Lord, and have built within us a capacity for intimate, personal, communion with Him. Therefore, by divine creative intention, it is not possible for us to find spiritual satisfaction or fulfillment in anything less than a developing love-relationship with Him.

Three key "testimonies" reveal the progressive levels of spiritual growth to which the Bride has developed. Each of these three confessions of her spiritual condition sets the stage for the intervention of the Lord to draw her up the "stairs" to the next level. Her first testimony relates to her self-importance: "My Beloved is mine, *(then, as an afterthought)* and I am His" SS 2:16a.

In her second testimony, some progress is evident, for a partial change in her priorities has occurred. Now she is able to put Him first and say: "I am my Beloved's, *(but adds)* and my Beloved is mine" SS 6:3a. Although weakened, an element of self-centeredness still rules her priorities.

Her third testimony expresses a total change. The Lord has now become her all in all. "I am my Beloved's, and His desire is toward me" SS 7:10. Her self-life has been completely dealt with and no longer controls either her desires or her actions.

Notice the complete reversal of positions in the progression of these testimonies which represent her spiritual condition. In her first confession, "My Beloved is mine," she is serving the Lord for her own benefit. She admits that she loves the Lord because He gives her the things she wants. This reveals a selfish, or a self-serving attitude toward the Lord:

> **"Because** of the savour of Thy good ointments Thy name is as ointment poured forth, **therefore** do the virgins love Thee" SS 1:3.

Her request, "Stay me with flagons, comfort me with apples: for I am sick of love" SS 2:5, reveals that she views the Lord on a far lower plane of experience than He desires for her. He seeks her fellowship while she seeks that which He can supply to please her.

In her third testimony, she is able to say, "I am my Beloved's, and His desire is toward me." Finally, He has become the center of her life. Instead of possessing the Lord, she is possessed by Him. She has left the place of self-centeredness where she had tried to use the Lord for her own purposes. Now she has submitted her life to Him that she might live and move in continual fellowship and communion with Him. This has opened a way of entrance into His chambers where she might become a partaker with Him in the outworking of His plan and purpose for mankind, now and in the ages to come.

Often, in the beginnings of our Christian experience we are spiritually satisfied because of the blessings we receive, and are content to rest in these. As we begin to grow spiritually, we are introduced by the Holy Spirit to the Person Who gives all of these blessings to us. As we fellowship with Him, He will gently correct *(chasten)* us in order to lead us beyond our initial experience in which we were content with receiving things from Him. Now we find our satisfaction in giving ourselves to Him, and together, in our being available for the building up of others.

During this initial state of our spiritual life, when our experiences were centered upon receiving from the Lord, we expressed our appreciation, telling the Lord that we "loved" Him. This love however, related to, and was the direct result of the blessings we were receiving. The center of our relationship to the Lord was in our "getting." As we grew spiritually, this expression of love took a different direction. Our "love" for the Lord began to center upon Him as a Person, which resulted in a desire to bring others into the same experience we had received from Him. Now the center of our relationship to the Lord has changed to "giving."

There are three different Greek words that are used to express this one English word, "love." The first, or lowest Greek word for "love" is "Eros." This word expresses a one-way love that moves toward us. It is a love that seeks self-gain. It is carnal or sensual, the lowest form of love. This Greek word for "love" is not used in the Bible.

The second Greek word for "love" is "Phileo." This word expresses the highest type of human love. This is a "love" that is reciprocated, or responds to love. "I love the Lord because He first loved me." This is a mutual love that flows two ways.

The third, and highest Greek word for "love" is "Agape." This is the word that is used to express divine love, and speaks of sacrifice. "For God so loved the world, that He gave His only begotten Son" John 3:16a. This word, "agape," expresses a one-way love. It is an outgoing, selfless, giving love that looks for nothing in return.

In the New Testament there is an illustration of the use of the latter two words for love: "phileo" and "agape." John 21:15-18 gives the account of Jesus restoring Peter, after Peter had denied Him. The Lord asked Peter, "Lovest thou Me more than these?" And Peter replied, "Yea, Lord; Thou knowest that I love Thee." Jesus repeated, "Lovest thou Me?" and Peter said, "Yea, Lord; Thou knowest that I love Thee." And then, the third time, Jesus said, "Lovest thou Me?" and Peter was grieved, and responded, "Lord, Thou knowest all things; Thou knowest that I love Thee."

The unfolding of Peter's confession that led to his grief, is quite different in the expression of the Greek language than is revealed in English. Peter had previously told the Lord, "Though I should die with Thee, yet will I not deny Thee" Matt 26:35a. But, when Jesus was taken captive and stood before the high priest to be judged, Peter denied he even knew Him because he feared for his own life.

After the resurrection, Jesus came to Peter and said, "Peter, do you *agape* (love to the point of death) Me?" And Peter said, "Lord, I *phileo* (am fond of) You." Before, Peter had said to Jesus, "Lord, I *agape* You (I will die for You)." But, when the trial came, Peter failed. He discovered that he was not all that he thought himself to be. Now, he could not use the word "agape" because his experience was less than his confession. Therefore, he had to speak from the level of his experience, so he said, "Lord, I *phileo* You."

Again Jesus said, "Peter, do you *agape* Me?" And Peter said, "Lord, You know that I *phileo* You." Then, Jesus came down to the level of Peter's experience and said, "Peter, do you *phileo* Me?" At this Peter broke and cried saying, "Lord, You know all things; You know that I *phileo* You." Because the Lord condescended to Peter's level of experience, his resistance to the Lord melted and he rose up into a new level of faith, fully restored.

We all desire the highest. However, each of us must start at the lowest where the Lord first found us and climb, step upon step, toward His chambers, gradually developing the capacity to enter within and partake of the highest expression of His love. Thus, the Bride in her first confession revealed her spiritual condition at that time when she said, "My Beloved is mine." This brought her to the lowest *(eros)* step on the stairs. She was only capable of responding selfishly to a one-way love, which flowed toward her.

The Lord began to bring about changes within her so she would be able to love *(phileo)* Him as a Person rather than loving *(eros)* Him because of all the things He was able to provide for her. After He tenderly corrected her, she was able to say in her second confession, "I am my Beloved's, and my Beloved is mine." She had progressed upward on the stairs to the "phileo" level of experience. She was responding to His love, and began to notice Him as a Person, but was still very interested in all of the blessings and gifts that were available to her.

Finally, He drew her further up the stairs toward the level of spiritual maturity where she was able to say "I am my Beloved's, and His desire is toward me." Now her love *(agape)* has become an outgoing love with no expectancy of return. The Lord has become her all in all, and she has entered into an abiding oneness in Him in which she shares His love *(agape)* that reaches out to the world. In undivided submission, devotion, and rest, she has reached the place in her spiritual growth where she is able to move with Him in ministry to the needs of others, or abide alone with Him in intimate communion. Therefore, He is able to say to her,

> "Come, My beloved, let us go forth into the field; let us lodge in the villages. Let us get up early to the vineyards; let us see if the vine flourish, whether the tender grape appear, and the pomegranates bud forth: there will I give thee My loves" SS 7:11-12.

Suddenly, all of the pain and loss she had to endure to become His Bride has faded into nothingness. She only sees the vineyard that is before them. Together, they will go forth into this vineyard to minister to others in love, while experiencing new dimensions of communion together.

> ". . . there will I give thee My loves" SS 7:12c.

Chapter 3

Our Spiritual Potential

The methods which the Lord uses to bring us into the level of spiritual maturity that He desires for us are progressively laid out, step upon step, within the Song of Solomon. These spiritual principles are available to, and will work for, those who prayerfully seek them out, and who sincerely desire to apply them to their lives.

As we experientially identify ourselves with the Bride, and partake with her in the many reductions that she experiences in qualifying to become His Bride, we also will be changed and become one with those who will emerge as His Bride at the coming "marriage supper of the Lamb."

> "And he saith unto me, Write, Blessed are they which are called unto the marriage supper of the Lamb. And he saith unto me, These are the true sayings of God" Rev 19:9.

Even though her first testimony, "He is mine," indicated that she was very immature and quite selfish, the Bridegroom longed to make her His Bride. It is encouraging to know that any "seeming" deficiency in our spirituality will not hinder the Lord from drawing us to Himself. This can be seen in the initial steps that were taken by the Bridegroom to establish a personal relationship with His potential Bride, despite her self-serving responses to Him. This process began as He sought to draw her to Himself by expressing His love for her through His "Song of Songs" SS 1:1.

The Bride responded to His Song of Love by expressing her desire for intimate communion with Him,

> "Let Him kiss me with the kisses of His mouth: for Thy love is better than wine" SS 1:2.

But she spoiled the beauty of this expression by stating the reason for her love:

> "**Because** of the savour of Thy good ointments Thy name is as ointment poured forth, **therefore** do the virgins love Thee" SS 1:3.

Notice the self-centeredness that is exposed through her response: "The reason I love you is because of the many things with which you bless me." However, the Lord looked beyond her present immaturity to the sincere hunger of her heart which she had expressed to Him in her prayer, "Draw me, we will run after Thee" SS 1:4a. Understanding this, He responded to her true need rather than to her present desires.

Anticipating the time when she would desire Him apart from anything He might do for her, He began to gently guide her toward the entrance to the stairs that would lead her upward into His chambers. He knew that as she matured spiritually, her desires and expressions would change and become more pleasing to Him. Then He Himself would become the center of her life, rather than the many superficial things she presently sought.

Our testimony often reveals our spiritual condition. Also, it expresses some of the hindrances to our spiritual maturity, just as the Bride's confession to the

Daughters of Jerusalem revealed the reason for her lack of spiritual growth.

> "I am black, but comely, O ye Daughters of Jerusalem, as the tents of Kedar, as the curtains of Solomon. Look not upon me, because I am black, because the sun hath looked upon me: my mother's children were angry with me; they made me the keeper of the vineyards; **but mine own vineyard have I not kept"** SS 1:5-6.

The vineyard is a type of the Body of Christ; He is the vine, we are the branches. These branches must be properly joined to the vine as their continuing life and health is dependent upon the strength they draw from it.

The problem is that the Bride has attached herself to "another" branch *(the Daughters of Jerusalem)* rather than to the vine *(Bridegroom)*. In effect she is saying, "I have centered my life in those who represent the Lord *("my mother's children")*, and have labored long and hard for them, even in the heat of the day *(sunburned)*. Then I realized that although I had worked more diligently than others, I was neglecting my own vineyard." She has come to realize that working for the Lord, even with intense zeal, cannot please Him or satisfy the spiritual hunger that is within her.

Notice that she charged "my mother's children" *(those who were very close to her)* as being angry with her. The Lord may use unexpected methods to provoke feelings of restlessness within us, that we may move away from lesser dependencies and begin our solitary ascent up the stairs toward His chambers. Thus, we must avoid judging or criticizing ministries *("the Watchmen" SS 5:7a)*, or other Christians *(the Daughters of Jerusalem)*, whom the Lord uses to produce this discomfort within us.

Recognizing her spiritual barrenness, she cried out to the Lord,

> **"Tell me**, O Thou Whom my soul loveth, where
> Thou feedest, where Thou makest Thy flock to rest
> at noon: for why should I be as one **that turneth
> aside** by the flocks of Thy companions?" SS 1:7.

She had become so busy and self-reliant that she
has failed to recognize His voice as He attempts to
direct her path to Himself. Now the Lord has arrested
her attention and she is ready to listen.

She has learned that she needs "something" more
than just being blessed by the overflow of someone
else's experience *("the flocks of Thy companions")*. She
understands that being fed by the testimony, or ministry of another is not sufficient to meet her deepest
need. She has come to the place in her spiritual development where she realizes that it is essential for her to
personally and intimately know the Lord. She must
abide in Him, or die.

With intense desire, she longs to know what she
should do, and asks the Lord for guidance:

> "Tell me" SS 1:7a.

He quickly answers her,

> "If thou know not, O thou fairest among women, go
> thy way forth by the footsteps of the flock, and feed
> thy kids beside the shepherds' tents" SS 1:8.

He instructs her to search out those who truly know
Him. The "footsteps of the flock" are those who are of
"like spirit" to Him. These walk with Him and have an
understanding of His ways. She is to find and follow
them, as they will lead her to Him *("the shepherds'
tent")*, rather than to themselves.

The intense spiritual hunger that is stirring the
Bride at this time has captivated the Lord's attention.
Her enlightened, expressed desire to personally know

Him has caused Him to turn aside from the "Daughters of Jerusalem" to seek her alone as His potential Bride. She has come to the place in her spiritual growth where she is determined to intently follow after Him. Because of her newly acquired **singular** desire toward Him, the Lord has reciprocated by singularly turning His interest toward her. Now He will begin to cultivate a special relationship with her. His "approbation" *(Divine favor)* now rests upon her.

> "There are . . . virgins without number. My dove, My undefiled is but one" SS 6:8-9a.

Therefore, He spoke a very encouraging word to her:

> "I have compared thee, O My love, to a company of horses in Pharaoh's chariots" SS 1:9.

This becomes a very powerful and penetrating compliment when it is properly understood. Challenged by the **spiritual potential** *("a company of horses")* that had been inactive, or dormant within her, the Lord revealed His intention to bring forth from within her, the very best.

Pharaoh was the greatest of the world's rulers at that time. His agents were sent throughout the known world to seek immature ponies that would be qualified to be hitched to Pharaoh's magnificent gold-overlaid chariot. From among these, the horses that would pull his chariot were prepared through intense, progressive training and discipline. At special times, these carefully chosen horses were hitched to the chariot of the king. Then in a beautiful demonstration of beauty, harmony, and unity, they brought forth the king into full view, displaying him in all of his regal glory.

> "For many are called, but few are chosen" Matt 22:14.

Thus, the Lord is telling the Bride that He has seen within her the quality and the potential that will enable her to successfully respond to His training and discipline. By submitting herself to the necessary process of qualification, she will be prepared to become a part of the company that will bring forth the King of kings in all of His beauty, majesty, and sovereign glory in the coming day of His manifestation and power.

The Lord elaborated further concerning this **potential** that He had seen to be within her and said,

> "Thy cheeks are comely with rows of jewels, thy neck with chains of gold. We will make thee borders of gold with studs of silver" SS 1:10-11.

Gold is a type of the divine nature, the "image" of our Lord Jesus Christ. Silver speaks of righteousness or right living, and jewels enhance beauty.

Here is set forth the character and the beauty that our Heavenly Bridegroom desires in His Bride. He intends to make her conformable to His image ("Gold") and likeness ("Silver"). Then in confidence, He will be able to present her, His Bride, in open view before mankind, as a witness ("Jewels") of His nature and character.

The Bride responded with disbelief to His expression of insight and encouragement concerning the potential that He saw within her. She did not feel she was worthy or capable of all that He said about her. Therefore, she replied,

> "Behold, Thou art fair, my Beloved, yea, pleasant: also our bed is green. The beams of our house are cedar, and our rafters of fir" SS 1:16-17.

The cedar and fir tree was common in this area. Apparently, her house was ordinary and her bedroom plain ("our bed is green"). She is saying, "Lord, this potential that you see within me, that of royalty, and of becoming righteous, seems beyond me. I am a simple, ordinary person without any special qualities or abilities. I have very little to offer."

Then she added,

"I am *(but)* a rose of Sharon, and a lily of the valleys" SS 2:1 ASV.

There were multiplied thousands of these covering the hillsides and the valleys. "I am just one of so many, Lord. Why should You single me out *(His approbation, or favor)*? Lord, what do You see in me?" The power and contrast in His reply to her is both penetrating and beautiful.

"As the **Lily among thorns**, so is My love **among** the Daughters" SS 2:2.

He is saying to her (and to us): "You may be as you say, but I saw the hunger of your heart. I was moved by your determination to obediently respond to Me when you first prayed 'Draw me'; and by your willingness to change your ways when you said 'Tell me.' You were expressing a longing for 'something' more than your present experience, and it turned My heart and desire toward you."

Even though she had no apparent human ability, beauty, or talents, the Lord saw the spiritual hunger and potential that was within her, and began to draw her to Himself as His Bride. These "seeming" limitations were not a hindrance to the Lord at all. Rather, He saw these as a challenge to bring forth the highest and best from the dormant spiritual capacity that lay within her.

He had said, "As the lily among thorns, so is My love among the Daughters." This is a beautiful and intense comparison. He saw her as being more desirable than all others, but to this she responded,

> "As the apple tree among the trees of the wood, so is My Beloved among the sons" SS 2:3a.

An apple tree is plain and unattractive, but its fruit is a delight to the physical senses. She is telling the Lord that she sees Him as being like this apple tree, because she greatly desires the blessings and the gifts *(apples)* that He is able to give her. Therefore she adds,

> "Stay me with flagons, comfort me with apples: for I am sick of love" SS 2:5.

She possesses an intense spiritual hunger, but has misappropriated its intended purpose. Rather than waiting for spiritual fulfillment, she still seeks a present satisfaction through natural means.

This was a poor comparison, but the best she is capable of expressing at this time in her relationship to Him. Even so, He was pleased with her progress and continued to give her all that she desired, because He recognized that she had said it out of the sincerity of her heart. Afterwards, she testified about His continued goodness to her:

> "I sat down under **His shadow** with great delight, and His fruit was sweet to my taste" SS 2:3b.

She had come into a feeling of satisfaction and rest, and spoke of the comfort of "His shadow." The Lord had met her need, and she was seemingly satisfied with the blessings she had received, even though she is only able to relate to His shadow at this time. She did not understand that His "shadow" was far less than the reality of His presence.

> "He brought me to the banqueting house, and His banner over me was love" SS 2:4.

Now that she has come into a time of rest, the Lord patiently waits for her to come to the understanding that she was created for much more than these blessings which He is able to give her in abundance. During this critical time, He continued to declare His love to her, and in anticipation, awaited her response. He longs for us to vocally respond to His desire for our companionship. Therefore, He restricted all who could distract her, that she might discover her need to come to Him alone.

> "I charge you, O ye Daughters of Jerusalem, by the roes, and by the hinds of the field, that ye stir not up, nor awake My love, **till she please**" SS 2:7 *("she" NAS margin)*.

The Lord is saying to all *(including counselors)* who were around her: "Do not try to please or satisfy her. It is My intention that she will become dissatisfied with her present feelings of fulfillment and of being content with all the blessings I have given her. I long for her to seek after Me for Myself."

There is a foundational spiritual principle expressed in "The Sermon on the Mount" that applies to the Bride's spiritual need at this time.

> "Blessed are the poor in spirit *(those who have come to the end of all self-seeking)*: for theirs is the Kingdom of Heaven *(the higher realm in God)*" Matt 5:3.

If we are satisfied with our present level of spiritual understanding and growth, the Lord will leave us there. The responsibility for entering the next step is upon us, for He had said concerning her, "Do not stir up, nor awake My love **until she please**." When we are ready to cry out to be led to the Lord Himself *(the Shepherd's tent)*, He will respond and begin to personally reveal Himself to us, and take us further.

As the Bride continued to rest within the banqueting house, satisfied with the many things she had received, the Lord continued to speak to her concerning His desire to make Himself known to her (SS 2:4). This caused a gradual awakening within her, and she began to desire Him above all else. Finally, she recognized His presence and cried out,

> **"The voice of my Beloved!** behold, He cometh leaping upon the mountains, skipping upon the hills" SS 2:8.

Her excited response stirred Him to begin the next step in preparing her to become His Bride. He withdrew Himself and stood in the shadows, outside of the "banquet room" of her present experience. She is yet incapable of realizing that His seeming withdrawal is actually a blessing that is intended to bring her up another step, upon which the experience of His manifest presence will be made available to her.

> "My Beloved is like a roe or a young hart: behold, He standeth behind our wall, He looketh forth at the windows, shewing Himself through the lattice" SS 2:9.

Hoping that she will notice Him, the Bridegroom began to show Himself through the lattice. He, the Lord of Glory, reluctantly remains without, alone and lonely, longing for her fellowship, while she is within, alone but comfortable, satisfied with all the blessings He has provided. He waits for her to realize that she had been redeemed for a higher purpose, and greatly desires that she will invite Him to come within, that they might commune and sup together.

> "Because thou sayest, I am rich, and increased with goods, and have need of nothing . . . Behold, I stand at the door, and knock: if any man hear My voice, and open the door, I will come in to him, and will sup with him, and he with Me" Rev 3:17a, 20.

This passage in Revelation expresses this same desire of the Lord for our fellowship. The Lord is not satisfied when we are content to abide merely in the area of His shadow. He longs to bring us into the experiential reality of His Person and presence, where He will be able to reveal Himself to us.

> "He that hath My commandments, and keepeth them, he it is that loveth Me: and he that loveth Me shall be loved of My Father, and I will love him, and will **manifest** Myself to him" John 14:21.

This word "manifest" means to make visible to one or more of our five natural senses. His manifest presence begins at the point where we pass from the "letter" of the Word into the "spirit" of the Word. It speaks of "sacred ground" within His chambers.

When we enter His manifest presence, He may lead us to quietly wait upon Him. He may make known to us something He desires to accomplish, and show us our part in its outworking. He may give us a special insight in His Word. Or, He may share with those who have experienced in some measure, "the fellowship of His sufferings" Phil 3:10b, a specific burden of prayer or intercession. The possibilities are manifold.

The Lord has been hurt so many times by those who take His presence lightly that He is reluctant to openly reveal Himself. Therefore, He will approach us very cautiously *("shewing Himself through the lattice")* to see if we are really interested in Him as a Person.

> "Behold, He standeth behind our wall, He looketh forth at the windows, shewing Himself through the lattice" SS 2:9b.

He longingly looks through the window, seeking to attract the attention of the Bride to see if she truly desires His fellowship. Finally, when she faintly notices

His face *(as a shadow through the window)*, she realizes that she can no longer remain satisfied with her present experience.

In full anticipation of all that is about to follow, she invites Him to come within. Her experience of coming to know Him in His manifested presence is about to begin.

The Lord's response to this "open door" was immediate.

> "My Beloved spake, and said unto me, Rise up, My love, My fair one, and come away" SS 2:10.

He has something far better to offer her, if she will "Rise up" with Him into a higher realm of spiritual reality. To this He added a word of encouragement concerning all that will take place as she responds to this upward call.

> "For, lo, the winter is past, the rain is over and gone; the flowers appear on the earth; the time of the singing of birds is come, and the voice of the turtle is heard in our land" SS 2:11-12.

The Bride has made a major breakthrough, as "the winter is past." "Winter" speaks of a time of barrenness in our spiritual experience in which the Lord is seemingly absent *(waiting without but looking within)*, and where there is little or no "moving" or "quickening" presence of the Holy Spirit. The past spiritual attainments of the Bride will seem to her as being a "barren winter" compared to all the Lord is about to make available to her as she progressively responds to His upward call.

Our spiritual growth is dependent upon our receiving from the Lord an impartation of "Spirit and Life." As we experience His manifest presence (**"Taste** *and see that the LORD is good" Ps 34:8a)*, we will receive this impartation of "Spirit and Life." This process is depicted here as the flowers appearing; the singing of birds; and the voice of the turtle being heard.

The "flowers appear*(ing)*" speaks of fruit that results from our growth into spiritual maturity. The "singing of birds" speaks of the expression of our worship that flows up to the Lord from deep within us. The "voice of the turtle" speaks of our becoming prophetic and giving anointed, vocal expression to His Word.

These spiritual qualities are not developed by an intellectual comprehension of His Word, but rather through an anointed impartation of His life to us—as the vine imparting its life into the branch. Only then can the spiritual truths which have become an experiential reality within us be rightly understood and communicated to others. It is essential that we invite the Lord to come within us and give Him full control of both the natural and spiritual areas of our lives.

Any amount of spiritual indifference that may be resident within us, along with a self-serving attitude that we have toward the Lord, will be exposed through our identification with the successive experiences of the Bride in becoming one with the Bridegroom. As we witness the correction of these problem areas within her, we will gain an understanding that will help us to submit to His dealings in our lives. Then He will be able to lead us, step upon step, up the stairs into a deeper experience of communion and cooperation with Him.

> "He made known His ways unto Moses, His acts unto the children of Israel" Ps 103:7.

It is one thing to observe what the Lord is doing; it is another to understand and become involved with Him in the outworking of all He intends. Paul's longing to be a partaker in "the fellowship of His sufferings" was evidenced in his cry,

"That I may know Him, and the power of His resurrection, and the fellowship of His sufferings, being made conformable unto His death" Phil 3:10.

The Lord longs to bring us into a higher realm of identification and experience *("that I may know Him")*, but the price is high. It requires our being identified with Him in death *("the power of His resurrection")* before we will be able to respond to Him in life *("the fellowship of His sufferings")*.

"My Beloved spake, and said unto me, Rise up, My love, My fair one, and come away" SS 2:10.

As we respond to His call to "rise up and come away," the Lord will lead us into this realm of experiential identification with Him; a higher experience where we as His Bride will come to know and love Him as never before.

And, along with this, we will have a part with Him in what He is about to do in the earth in our day.

Nothing that we could ever obtain apart from Him can compare with this.

Chapter 4

A Single Eye

"Behold, thou art fair, My love;
behold, thou art fair;
thou hast doves' eyes" SS 1:15.

"My Beloved spake, and said unto me, Rise up,
My love, My fair one, and come away" SS 2:10.

"The King hath brought me
into His chambers" SS 1:4b.

The Bridegroom has seen within the Bride a quality that has attracted His singular attention toward her. She has a "single eye" which is focused upon Him. Therefore, He sees her in a different relationship to Himself than the many Daughters of Jerusalem. His favor, or approbation now rests upon her as He begins the process of drawing her, as His Bride, unto Himself.

There are two different levels of relationship in our spiritual development. The first is to find its outworking within us. Deep within each one of us is a "chamber" which we are to make ready and into which we, "as a Bride," are to receive our Heavenly Bridegroom, the Lord Jesus Christ, for quality times of fellowship with Him.

"Behold, I stand at the door, and knock: if any man hear My voice, and open the door, I will come in to him, and will sup with him, and he with Me" Rev 3:20.

The second is to find its outworking within His Throne. Here, "as an overcomer" *(matured son)* we are brought up into the chamber which He has prepared, the Throne of the resurrected and ascended Lord Jesus Christ.

> "To him that overcometh will I grant **to sit with Me** in My Throne, even as I also overcame, and am set down with My Father in His Throne" Rev 3:21.

Corresponding to these two areas of relationship are two levels of experience in our identification with the Lord.

The first finds its fulfillment within the "Chamber of our Heart." Through our devotion and submission to the Son, we experientially relate to Him as a Bride.

As we respond to the seeking presence of our Heavenly Bridegroom and open our spirit unto Him, He will enlarge the spiritual capacity that is within us. This will result in our having the ability to enter into and enjoy quality times of personal fellowship and communion with our Lord, as His Bride.

> "He that hath the Bride is the Bridegroom" John 3:29a.

The second is experienced in the "Chamber of His Throne." Through our overcoming obedience and cooperation with the Son, we are raised up into a place of identification with Him as a son.

As our times of "overcomings" begin to outweigh our "shortcomings," we develop toward spiritual maturity. This increase in our spiritual capacity will enable the Lord to impart to us an understanding of the principles and workings of His Kingdom, and will equip us for participation with Him in His Throne, as a son.

"If we suffer, we shall also reign with Him" 2 Tim 2:12a.

These "chambers" represent the ground upon which we meet with and interact with our Lord Jesus Christ. They metaphorically refer to our redemptive relationship to Him: as a Bride, and as a son. In order to properly function in these parallel relationships, there must be resident within us an active, abiding sensitivity to His presence, and to His voice. This will require of us a settled, determined "set" in our spirit toward fully knowing and obeying Him.

The key to our entering into the full outworking of these two different areas of experience is to fully open our heart to the Lord Jesus and express to Him our love, our trust, and our desire to obey Him. In response, He will meet us within the chamber of our heart, so that we as a Bride may enjoy times of intimate communion with Him. At other times He will lead us, as a son, into the area of His Throne *(chamber)* where we will be enabled to participate with Him in the outworking of His purposes toward mankind.

"And if children, then heirs; heirs of God, and joint-heirs with Christ; if so be that we suffer with Him, that we may be also glorified together" Rom 8:17.

The Song of Solomon reveals to us the methods by which the Lord prepares us for these areas of experiential relationship with Him. These progressive, "step upon step" dealings are arranged by the Lord to produce within us that level of spiritual maturity and integrity which will enable us to become both compatible with, and productive in, our being seated with Him in His Throne—as a Bride, and as a son.

We will never be qualified to "rule" with Him (Rev 2:26-27; 5:10; 20:6) until we have first fully submitted ourselves to Him, as His Bride. Therefore, our initial seeking should be centered in our being prepared to become His Bride.

> "Let us rejoice and be exceeding glad, and let us give the glory unto Him: for the marriage of the Lamb is come, and **His wife hath made herself ready**. And it was given unto her that she should **array herself** in fine linen, bright and pure: for the fine linen is the righteous acts of the saints. And he saith unto me, Write, Blessed are they that are bidden to the marriage supper of the Lamb" Rev 19:7-9a ASV.

This special time of preparation in becoming His Bride will begin as we so completely fall in love with Jesus that our fervent expressions of love stir Him to become singularly interested in us.

> "While the King sitteth at His table, my spikenard sendeth forth the smell thereof" SS 1:12.

This continuing upward flow of the "fragrance" of our love for Him will result in our Heavenly Bridegroom taking special notice of us, apart from all others. He will respond to this expression of our love for Him and, in return, assure us of His love for us.

> "Behold, thou art fair, My love; behold, thou art fair; thou hast doves' eyes" SS 1:15.

The fact that the Lord so intimately responds to the worshipful expression of our love for Him is a mystery that we can little comprehend, but marvelously experience. We should consider His seeing us as a "lily among thorns" SS 2:2, as being a compliment beyond comparison. Now in confidence, we can cooperate with Him as He calls us apart for the processings which will perfect us to become His Bride.

> "Arise, My love, My fair one, and come away. O My dove, that art in the clefts of the rock, **in the secret places of the stairs**" SS 2:13b-14a.

The Bride has entered into a very special relationship with the Lord in her spiritual experience. Because of her single eye toward Him, He has begun the process of separating her unto Himself. He has placed her "in the clefts of the rock, in the secret *places* of the stairs."

"Stairs" provide a means of ascent from one level to a higher one. These stairs, and the secret entrance to them, are hidden to all, except the Lord makes known the way. They lead into His chambers where He desires to bring us for times of intimate communion and fellowship with Him. Also, the stairs speak of the processings of the Lord which He places in our path. A right response to these will result in our becoming an overcomer. This will produce within us a level of spiritual maturity and integrity which will enable us to become spiritually productive in our relationship to Him, in His Throne.

In order for us to come into these realms of communion *(Bride)* and cooperative experience *(Son)* with our Heavenly Bridegroom, we must not settle for less than the development within us of a "single eye" which has clear focus and discernment. Having this single eye is essential so these "stairs" will become clearly visible and accessible to us.

> "The eyes of your understanding being enlightened; that ye may know what is the hope of His calling, and what the riches of the glory of His inheritance in the saints" Eph 1:18.

Notice that the Lord called her His "Dove." A dove is similar to a pigeon, but a dove has a very unusual quality—it has a single eye. That is, it does not have side vision. For this reason, doves are often referred to as "love birds." When a dove sets its gaze upon another dove, it sees nothing else, nor is it easily distracted. Its eye is single.

Our having a single eye for the Lord *("O My dove"),* will release Him to impart to us the necessary spiritual perception which will enable us to enter these stairs and begin our ascent upward toward His chambers.

David came to a time in his experience when he cried out,

> "One thing have I desired of the LORD, that will I seek after" Ps 27:4a.

All of David's drives and ambitions had been reduced to the expression of this single desire: "One thing . . . that I may dwell in the house of the LORD all the days of my life, to behold the beauty of the LORD, and to inquire in His temple" Ps 27:4. David, who knew he was to become king over Israel, was a man with many desires. Yet, through the acquired vision of a single eye, he was able to cry out from the depths of his being, "One thing have I desired of the LORD."

The Lord desires to bring us into this same experience of having a single eye for Him. We were created with this ability to focus our desires. Our inner man, quickened and inhabited by the Holy Spirit through the new birth, has a newly created capacity to respond to His presence, and to come to know Him intimately. All we need do is to become willing to lift our spirit toward Him. One of the greatest miracles of creation is that an infinite and mighty God finds great pleasure and satisfaction in His times of fellowship with us, mere finite beings.

It is here that we find our true fulfillment. Our completion is in Him; it is not possible for us to become complete apart from Him. It should be perfectly natural and normal for us, as a new creation, to move into "the deeper things of God" and to enjoy His manifest presence and fellowship. We were created for this. When He sees that we long for His friendship and that we are determined to develop a single eye toward Him, the Lord will come to us and say, "O My Dove." This will be as music to our inner being.

"O My dove, that art in the clefts of the rocks" SS 2:14a.

Once we have stirred His desire toward us, He will gently place us within these clefts in the rock. This is a specially prepared environment, where He comes and progressively changes us, according to our desire toward Him.

This "Rock" is the Lord Jesus Christ Himself. Through direct intervention *("clefts")*, He will become active on our behalf and begin to remove from us, and from our surroundings, all that hinders our relationship to Him. It is His determined purpose to "make us" one with Him, as His Bride. He alone is the Rock Foundation upon which we are to be built and established.

When I first began to seek after the Lord with the desire to intimately know Him, I received an inner sense of knowing the "Rock" was there, but buried deep beneath the rubble that had accumulated during my lifetime, apart from Him. Then it was revealed to me that this rubble was separating me from the Lord I greatly desired to know. This caused an urgency within me to begin removing all of this rubble from my life that I might stand firmly upon the Rock.

As we begin to view the Lord with a single eye, He will place within us a strong desire for a washing, or cleansing of our being. As we progressively dig down to the stratum of Rock upon which we will be able to firmly stand, the Lord will empower us to forever dispose of the "rubble" that has accumulated in our lives. Now the Lord will be able to reveal to us a new basis for our identity with Him. Instead of standing upon the rubble and debris of many frustrating failures, there will come into our being the Rock Foundation assurance that the Lord will continue His work of fully changing us into the Bride that He desires, as we continue in our times of fellowship with Him.

John the Baptist said, "He must increase, but I must decrease" John 3:30. In effect he is saying "the way up is down." In order to find the place of entrance to these stairs, we must first dig down through this accumulated rubble to the Rock. Here, the cleft in the Rock will become apparent to us. We will be able to enter and begin our ascent. As we progress upward, the Lord will become more personal and real to us. We will begin to see and understand things from the perspective in which the Lord sees them.

In the beginning of the Song of Solomon, the Lord saw a potential or quality within His intended Bride and said, "I have compared thee, O My love, to a company of horses in Pharaoh's chariots" SS 1:9.

Now He is ready to take her a step further, and tells her, "O My dove, that art in the clefts of the rock." These "clefts" in the rock speak of "openings" which give the Lord access, or the "right" to move into our lives. Here, we are separated from among the Daughters of Jerusalem as the Lord becomes singularly interested in us. As we give Him permission to work within us as He chooses and encourage Him to do so, we will be progressively changed into the Bride that He intends us to become.

Another quality that the Lord desires to develop within us is stability. Once we have become free from all of the rubble and rubbish that separated us from Him, He will carefully "set" us within this "cleft in the Rock." As we rest there, His presence will become as a song (SS 1:1) as He expresses to us His desire to hear our song of love and worship.

> "Let Me see thy countenance, **let Me hear** thy voice; for sweet is thy voice, and thy countenance is comely" SS 2:14b.

Now we will be able, with a pure heart and a single eye, to sing our song of love and worship back to Him. This will strengthen the security of our developing friendship with Him.

While resting in the warmth and comfort of His presence within the cleft of the Rock, the Lord may speak a word of admonition or correction to us. Whenever the Lord sees within us anything that could hinder the solidity of our new-found fellowship with Him, He will help us to recognize the problem. Then, with our cooperation, He will be free to deal with it. Thus, His admonition:

> "Take us the foxes, the little foxes, that spoil the vines: for our vines have tender grapes" SS 2:15.

A "fundamental urge of life" is resident within each one of us and manifests itself as a primary soul strength. Within this is the "law of self-preservation" which operates at the very root of our Adamic nature. Left to ourselves this law controls us, finding its expression through us in many diverse ways. The Lord must deal with this self-perpetuating soul-strength at its very root in order to bring us to the place where we will truly say, "Lord, I give up my right to my own life. I am totally Yours; You may do with my life AS YOU PLEASE. I understand what this means, and I will respond rightly as You accomplish within me all that You desire."

The experience of Job is a clear example of the power of this "law of self-preservation." The Lord allowed him to go through a series of testings in order to bring about the necessary correction. Satan came before the Throne and told the Lord that the only reason Job served Him was because of the blessings which he received. The Lord allowed Satan to remove these blessings from Job in order to reveal what he would do. Job's reaction was,

> "The LORD gave, and the LORD hath taken away; blessed be the Name of the LORD" Job 1:21b.

Here Job was still standing firmly on the Rock. The devil again came before the Lord and said, "The real interest of Job is his own flesh. If You touch his flesh, then he will curse You." The Lord then permitted Satan to touch Job's body, but he could not take his life.

In the next view of Job, he is sitting on the ash heap, covered with boils. His wife, friends, and comforters had turned against him, but again Job retained his integrity and his trust in the Lord. He came to the place to which we must come, to break this power of self-preservation and remove its place of control from our lives. Job cried out and said,

> "Though He slay me, yet will I trust in Him" Job 13:15a.

After this experience, Job was able to say,

> "I have heard of Thee by the hearing of the ear: but now mine eye seeth Thee" Job 42:5.

Job had been set free from his self-life, and was standing within the cleft of the Rock. Now he could clearly see the Lord Who had brought him into this place of vision and understanding.

A person's life can be pictured as a vessel. If a vessel becomes marred in a potter's hands while he is working on it, the potter reduces it to powder. Then he remakes it into something that is either useful, beautiful, or both, as he sees best. The problem is that we, as vessels in the hands of the Master Potter, are not always willing to allow Him to reduce our lives to powder so He can remake us as He chooses. We must implicitly trust Him, realizing that He will form us in such a way that it will bring forth the very best from the potential that He sees within us. If we are to enter "the secret of the stairs" and move upward upon them, we must be willing for this processing to take place. However, many of us have been reluctant to trust the Master Potter with our lives.

One time, the Lord visited us during chapel in a very unusual way. He prophetically revealed Himself to us as a master musician who greatly desired to hear a symphonic composition. But first, all of the instruments had to be tuned. The discordant sound was horrible as they were being brought into tune. Then the Lord indicated that this is how we sound to Him until we are brought into unity and harmony with Him. Therefore, He tolerates this terrible noise, knowing that once His instruments *(we)* are tuned, a harmonious symphony will resound in all of its beauty and power.

During this service, each of us were being tuned in order to bring forth this beautiful musical expression that He longed to hear. Then the scene changed as the Lord began to express the perplexity of His heart. He knew that some of the instruments were so badly out of tune that it would take a great deal of tension to bring them up to pitch. Also, He knew that if too much pressure was applied, the string might snap and that instrument would need to be set aside.

Then came a revelation of the broken heart of the Lord, knowing that the instrument might say, "If I have to submit to all this pressure, I will quit." If we are to go on to be identified with Him, we must come to the place where we will allow Him to put His finger on our lives and deal with this law of self-preservation that is within each one of us. We must come, as Job did, to this commitment, "Though He slay me, yet will I trust in Him." We must enter the cleft in the Rock, our Lord Jesus Christ, and allow Him to tune our lives, no matter what it takes, or how much pressure is needed to bring us into pitch.

> "O My dove, that art in the clefts of the rock, in the secret *places* of the stairs, let Me see thy countenance, **let Me hear thy voice**; for sweet is thy voice, and thy countenance is comely" SS 2:14.

The Lord greatly desires to bring forth a melody from within His Bride as He plays upon the strings of her heart. To accomplish this, He has reached into the very foundation of her being and removed all that could hinder their relationship, or provoke her to turn aside to another. As He gently brings the totality of her being into tune, her life is becoming as this expression of beautiful music to Him.

Now she can, with a single eye, respond to His presence as He visits her and worship Him through this harmony that has come into her life. Now He will be able to say to her in anticipation and in confidence,

> "Arise, My love, My fair one, and come away" SS 2:13b.

Chapter 5

Our Ascent Toward Him

"O My dove . . . LET ME SEE thy countenance,
LET ME HEAR thy voice"
SS 2:14a.

The Lord looks to see whether the poise of our spirit is upward toward Him; then He listens within the innermost part of our being to hear an unqualified "yes" to His desire to lead us further.

Our heart's desire toward the Lord ("Let Me See"), and the expression of our willingness to obey ("Let Me Hear") determines the action that the Lord will take to bring us into the full fruition of the potential He sees within us.

"If ye be willing and obedient, ye shall eat the good of the land" Is 1:19.

To be "willing" means that my self-life no longer controls my desires and actions. I have unconditionally yielded to the Lord the full control of my life, and all that pertains to it. Every part of my being desires the very best the Lord has for me.

To be "obedient" speaks of my having a "spirit of obedience" that is resident within me, and is responsive to His requests.

Therefore, I "wait upon the Lord" for His enabling "grace for obedience" to become both operative and effective within me. For this newly established heart-willingness to find its full outworking, it is crucial that I spend quality time actively "waiting upon the Lord." This will result in my having both the desire and the ability to become willingly obedient to Him.

> "By Whom we have received **grace** and apostleship, **for obedience** to the faith among all nations, for His Name" Rom 1:5.

Grace is the essential ingredient of the New Covenant.

> "A new heart also will I give you, and a new spirit will I put within you: and I will take away the stony heart out of your flesh, and I will give you an heart of flesh. And I will put My Spirit within you, and CAUSE *(grace)* you to walk in My statutes, and ye shall keep My judgments, and do them" Ezek 36:26-27.

Grace is the "divine empowering" that creates within me the desire and the ability to obey (Acts 1:8). This capability to daily abide in "a state of obedience" takes place as I continually exchange my inabilities and weaknesses for His strength and ability. This exchange will take place as I actively "wait upon Him."

> "He giveth power to the faint; and to them that have no might He increaseth strength. Even the youths shall faint and be weary, and the young men shall utterly fall: but **they that wait upon the LORD** shall renew *(exchange)* their strength; they shall mount up with wings as eagles; they shall run, and not be weary; and they shall walk, and not faint" Is 40:29-31.

When these qualities, "heart-willingness" *(our part)* and "grace for obedience" *(His part)* abide within us and work together in harmony, they will bring forth rich spiritual fruit within our lives.

> "If ye be willing and obedient, ye shall **eat** the good of the land" Is 1:19.

The "good of the land" of which the Lord is speaking, is that total "area" of my life which was brought under His authority when I relinquished all self-control to Him and made Him LORD of my life. Now, I must daily confirm His total control over my life and circumstances, both for my good, and for His higher purposes, even though this inevitably will have a drastic effect upon my comfort, and the desires of my self-life.

The secret of understanding how to approach and ascend the "stairs" will begin to unfold as I maintain a right attitude and response to these two words, "willing" and "obedient." Jesus expressed this same principle concerning heart-obedience when He said,

> "He that HATH My commandments, and KEEPETH them, he it is that loveth Me: and he that loveth Me shall be loved of My Father, and I will love him, and will manifest Myself to him" John 14:21.

> "If a man love Me, HE WILL KEEP MY WORDS: and My Father will love him, and We will come unto him, and make Our abode with him" John 14:23b.

There is a "key" that will unlock the door which leads to the upward path of the stairs.

> "O My dove, that art in the clefts of the rock, in the secret *places* of the stairs" SS 2:14a.

This "key" has to do with cultivating within the depth of my being a spirit of willing obedience. This maturing "heart-obedience" will increase as my love for the Lord grows and as I grow in the ability to trust my life in His hands. The right use of this "key" will enable me to cooperate with Him, as He leads me through the many "dealings" that are intended to change me into the Bride He desires.

As a consequence of this new found "willing obedience," an inner knowing that I have entered the process of becoming His Bride will become a reality within me and many spiritual rewards will ensue as a result of my heart-obedience to Him.

> "My Beloved spake, and said unto me, Rise up, My love, My fair one, and come away" SS 2:10.

As I respond to this expression of His desire toward me, and begin to climb the stairs, I must consider that a "stair" has first a riser and then a step, or platform. My ascent toward the Lord must progress one step at a time, ever upward toward Him, riser and step upon riser and step. The Lord awaits within His chambers, at the top of these stairs.

The first riser and step may be called "revelation." When a scripture is quickened within me, my understanding is "opened" concerning it. As I embrace this understanding *(the riser)* and act upon it *(the step)*, it will become a personal reality within my life experience.

Now I have come up the distance of the first riser *(the revelation)* and have experientially possessed the territory of the first step *(the revelation experienced)*. This will bring me to the next riser and step in the process of my spiritual growth. These stairs will direct my path ever upward toward His highest and best where I will have a part with Him in the unfolding and outworking of His ongoing purposes.

For example, the Song of Solomon became very real and personal to me through an unusual experience during a weekend outstation, while I was a student in

Bible School. The Lord had been stirring me to seek Him and I felt an intense spiritual hunger. After the evening meal in the home where we stayed, I retired to my room and propped myself upon the bed with some pillows. I opened my Bible to the Song of Solomon, and as I expressed my heart's desire to the Lord while reading, something began to happen which is difficult to describe. I was caught up, as it were, into the Song of Solomon. I became unaware of myself as the message of this book began to unfold within me.

I became uniquely identified with each one of its actors; the Bridegroom, the Bride, and the Daughters of Jerusalem. I experienced their desires, their feelings, and their interactions as they "lived" within me. I felt as they did. This lasted, perhaps for several hours, as I waited in the Lord's presence.

After this unusual anointing lifted, I realized that I had entered into a spiritual realm, or "opening," of understanding the Song of Solomon. My next thought was, "Now I have a revelation that I can teach." Immediately the Lord spoke to me, "When I open My Word, do not rush out and preach it. First, eat it, experience it, live it, and then minister the result." The Lord was telling me that the Word must become personalized and integrated into my life experience before I could share it with any understanding or authority.

Thus, the "riser" that had led me into this unfolding of Scripture was not enough in itself. It was necessary that I be subjected to the experience of divinely arranged circumstances that would cause this opening of the Word I had received to become a personal reality within me.

"For we are His workmanship, created in Christ Jesus unto good works, which **God hath before ordained** that we should walk in them" Eph 2:10.

65

These "good works" are the Lord's part whereby He creates upon the step that is above the riser, a set of circumstances which He arranges to bring us into a practical understanding of spiritual reality.

Then I began to comprehend the depth of all that was the divine intention when Jesus entered this world as a baby in order to identify Himself with man and experience all that man experiences.

> "Though He were a Son, yet LEARNED HE obedience by the things which He suffered; and being made perfect, HE BECAME the Author of eternal salvation unto all them that obey Him" Heb 5:8-9.

Jesus "learned obedience." He was led into the wilderness where He intensely hungered, but refused satisfaction until it was provided for Him by His Heavenly Father. Thus, He overcame all temptation to act on His own in order to satisfy His need. He had within Himself a determined "set of spirit" with an aptitude for learning how to please His Father which resulted in His being "willingly obedient."

The Word declares that Jesus was the Lamb which was slain "from the foundation of the world" Rev 13:8b. Redemption through Jesus had been completely accomplished in the will and purpose of God before the world was created *(Riser)*. Jesus emptied Himself of Deity, and through obedience BECAME the Author of our redemption *(Step)*.

That which He was eternally *(judicially)*, He became *(experientially)*. Through a total submission to the will of His Father, which was wrought out upon the anvil of His life experience, Jesus experientially qualified Himself to become the Author of our salvation. The "riser" expresses His judicial position according to the will of His Father. The "step" expresses the will of His Father being made an experiential reality within Him, thereby becoming His possession through experience.

We are given a picture of how Jesus was able to "learn" or experience these things.

> "Who, being in the form of God, thought it not robbery to be equal with God: but made Himself of no reputation, and took upon Him the form of a servant, and was made in the likeness of men" Phil 2:6-7.

Jesus was eternally in the form *(morpha)* of God, yet He took upon Himself the form *(morpha)* of man. He WAS God, but He did not come as God acting like a man; rather, He became a man, submitting Himself to the disciplines of life. In His condescension, there is no human heart or need that is too low for Him to reach.

Jesus, unlike Satan (see Is 14:13-14), did nothing of His own will, but only that which the Father sent Him to do. In each area of His life experience, in which He was tested while in the wilderness, Jesus refused to act out of His own will, or to seek His own good, and thereby overcame. He became the Author of our Salvation, not just because it was the will of God for Him (which it was) but because He qualified through His life experience to become our Savior.

Thus, to "work out your own salvation with fear and trembling" Phil 2:12b, means "that which is freely given to me" must be experientially worked into my life experience that I might become all the Lord desires me to be. The Word must become flesh within me so it can be openly demonstrated to the world through my life.

I had asked the Lord to "draw me." This led to an increased hunger and desire for the Lord which resulted in the "opening" of the Song of Solomon to me. As a result of this revelatory visitation from the Lord, I was brought to a higher level *(the top of the first riser)* of

67

spiritual revelation and understanding. But, there was more. The "revelation" that I received *(riser)* had to become a part of me and reflect Jesus through my daily pattern of life *(step)*.

As I arrived at the top of the riser to enter this "stage" of life experience, the step crossed the riser and appeared to me as being a cross. It rested on top of the revelation that had brought me upward this far and was situated so I could not enter the step that was beyond until first I embraced this cross. As I died further to my own ways, I was released to move into the circumstances the Lord had prearranged for me on this level. As these had their full effect upon me, the revelations I had received became within me a present reality, and "substance" was added to my spiritual experience.

> "Then said Jesus unto His disciples, If any man will come after Me, let him deny himself, and take up his cross, and follow Me. For whosoever will save his life shall lose it: and whosoever will lose his life for My sake shall find it" Matt 16:24-25.

The next riser became a test concerning my willingness to be obedient to the Lord. He used my previous revelation and experience *(the riser and step below)* as a means to test me. In submitting to this test, I learned through patient "suffering," as more of the energized self-will that remained within me was exposed. Again, as I embraced the cross at the top of this riser, a further (deeper) experience of dying to self became personalized within me and I moved up into yet another plateau of resurrection life and experience in Him.

This pattern of spiritual development and growth can be found in varied forms in each of our lives. As we continue to climb the stairs in our spiritual development and growth, we will be drawn upward on progressive "risers" of deepening revelation which will be personalized within us upon the next step. Following this, our present position will be tested through "diverse arrangements" placed in our path by the Lord for this purpose. Thus, it is imperative that we recognize and rightly respond to these.

The "spirit of obedience" which is birthed and strengthened through these progressive victories, as we ascend the stairs, will become an abiding reality and strength within us. The application of this to our spiritual experience will lead us toward an experiential identity with the Lord in "the fellowship of His sufferings." Now we are at the level of spiritual growth where we may become increasingly identified with Him in the outworking of His purposes (compare Phil 3:10 with SS 7:11-12).

Notice that Jesus said, "**If** any man will come after Me, let him . . . ." He used the word "IF" because the taking up of our cross is conditional. This cross is something we can either ignore, take up, or put down. It is within our ability to choose, or to reject our cross. Thus, a physical impairment is not a cross because we can neither take it up nor put it down.

The cross that we "choose" to bear has nothing to do with the "fact" of our salvation or with our going to heaven. We are saved and will go to heaven because Jesus bore HIS CROSS. If we are to grow into spiritual maturity and enter some "measure" of identification with the Lord in "the fellowship of His sufferings," then it becomes essential that we bear OUR CROSS, whatever it may be. This takes a determined action on our part.

> "If ye be willing and obedient, ye shall eat the good of the land" Is 1:19.

The cross the Lord uses on one individual is not identical to that of another because we differ greatly in our makeup. That which works to crucify me would not accomplish the same in another. For example, I was once in a situation in which my income had been provided. However, the Lord showed me that I was to work, regardless. At the same time, another young man who was also hungry for God needed an income; but he felt the Lord had indicated that he should not work. Because we were quite different in our makeup, the Lord used "working" to deal with my self-life; and He used "unemployment" to deal with his.

These two opposite means were used by the Lord to bring about the same result within each of us. Thus, we dare not say, "This is the way it worked for me," and then attempt to place our yoke upon another's neck. The Pharisees did this. They weighted people down and killed them by putting a legalistic yoke on them which they themselves could not bear. Your cross may be quite different from the cross that I am to carry. Our Lord was a carpenter, and He knows how to make a cross that will fit each of us. We must not interfere with the plan of God. In the outworking of these crosses, our own ideas often conflict with what the Lord knows to be best.

> "For we are His workmanship, created in Christ Jesus unto good works, which God hath before ordained that we should walk in them" Eph 2:10.

In order to bring about a further crucifixion within my life, to prepare me for the ministry that would come into being in His time, the Lord had to dig yet deeper within my life to deal with the "self-drives" that were within me. The law of "self-preservation" which works within each of us was very strong within me as I had owned two successful businesses. The Lord dealt with me to sell these and go to Bible School. Since I received a cash settlement, as well as a check each week for the next six years, my income was adequate. Therefore, I did not need to work while attending school. During this time, the Lord dealt with me about my weekly check. I was to give it to a young man for a missionary trip to South America. In obedience, I did so, and soon we were living on squash that we had picked up from the school dump.

A few weeks later, the Lord told me that I was to go to work. About three miles from the school, there was a furniture factory that made upholstered chair frames. They were unable to keep employees because they paid very low wages for extremely hard work. In obedience to the Lord, I applied and was hired at one dollar and five cents an hour. Night after night, I was so tired after working that I could barely drag myself to the car to get home and fall into bed.

The weather was bitter cold at this time. Often I was sent in a large truck to a secluded railroad siding where, with only the light of a lantern, I was to unload boxcars of hardwood lumber. Alone, cold, and tired, as I unloaded these boxcars night after night, my spirit sank lower and lower. Then I was asked to work one Saturday morning because a tractor-trailer load of lumber had arrived. At 7:30 I started unloading the lumber, outside in the cold, freezing rain. I felt weary, discouraged, and wished I could be home in bed. About 8:00, the owner came out and said, "No, no, that's not the way to do it. Step to one side and I will show you." He started to unload the lumber frantically, as fast as he could. Then he said, "Do it like that," and went inside to rest.

I thought of the money I was receiving each week from the sale of the businesses—much more than I needed to live on. Why was I here, tired and cold, unloading this lumber? I did not need this job! Also, I knew that the young man who was receiving my money

71

each week was home in bed, warm and comfortable. I literally began to react as this worked on me. The next step naturally would be to act on the thoughts that came to me. "All this is absolutely stupid. I am going to tell this man off and quit."

But I had told the Lord that I wanted all that He had for me—His highest and best. I had made many extravagant promises to the Lord, telling Him all I would do for Him. As I stood in the freezing rain upon that pile of unloaded lumber, an intense warfare raged within me. Then a verse from Job came to me, "Though He slay me, yet will I trust in Him," and I began to melt. I repeated this to the Lord and said, "Lord, I do not care what happens to me, I am going all the way with You." Just then, something of eternal value and substance was created deep within my being. I was changed. A deep inner peace, along with an imparted ability to obey the Lord developed within me, and I was able to finish unloading the truck. My commitment to the Lord was literally burned into the fiber of my being through the intensity of this situation.

Later, as I talked with the young man who was receiving the money, he said, "Saturday morning the strangest thing happened. I was in bed (which I knew) and the Lord began dealing with me to get up and pray for somebody. It was so strong that I just couldn't escape it, so I got out of bed. Then the Lord gave me a vision of someone in a truck and told me to intercede for him."

I said, "I know who that was!" and explained it to him. Now I truly understood it was the Lord Who brought me through this experience to reduce me inwardly so I would not react to Him in my own ways, that I might stand in the place of pressure. And through my obedience in this, a "Spirit of obedience," or an aptitude to obey the Lord was imparted into my being.

Within each one of us is a "potential" which the Lord desires to perfect. Therefore, He will carefully begin to tighten the "string" in order to tune it to the right pitch, that it may sound forth a pure note of "music" in all its beauty *(our acceptance of His will in the place of intense pressure)*. If this string were to snap as the pressure increased, all would be lost. However, in my case, the Lord had caused intercession to be made for me so it would not snap. Now I understood that I might have quit, collected my pay check and gone home, but I would have completely missed all the Lord desired to accomplish within me through that situation.

"O My dove, that art in the clefts of the rock." Now, within the security of His protection from which I cannot be shaken, I am enabled to stand and to go through the dealings of God. And now I am able to agree with Job, "Though He slay me, yet will I trust in Him." This is a law of spiritual growth. If we are to progress toward spiritual maturity, then the law of self-preservation that is embedded within each of us must be dealt with. Otherwise, the fleshly "I" will manifest itself in our spiritual walk, and in everything we do. The "I" that causes us to protect our self-image and our own well-being will assert itself and wreck His purposes for us unless it is dealt with. There is no easy way to accomplish this. Jesus said, "IF any man will come after Me, let him . . . ." Knowing that it will cost us everything, each of us must make this choice.

On yet another occasion, I had planned to visit a man who intimately knew the Lord, and was a spiritual father to me. The arrangements were made, and he had said there would be a special meal ready for me when I arrived. As I headed for the car, halfway between the house and the garage, the Lord clearly said, "You are not to go." I halted. I knew it was the Lord, but I reacted. My friend was expecting me at a certain time and would have the meal prepared. It was to be a very special time of spiritual fellowship. For weeks, I had been waiting with anticipation. With desire and expectancy, I planned to spend several days with him.

But the Lord had just said, "You are not to go." First came intense disappointment; then rebellion welled up, and I decided, "I will go anyway." I realized, however, what I was about to do. God had spoken, and this was a cross for me to accept and embrace. The intense desire to go had risen up within me and cut aCROSS (†) the Word of the Lord to me. But I knew that I had no choice except to obey. Finally, I melted and said, "All right, Lord, I will not go. I will call and tell him that I am not able to come."

As soon as I had accepted in my heart the verdict, and spoke it to the Lord, He said; "Now you may go, but you are not going alone. I am going with you, for you are now going in the center of My will and purpose." This trip became a turning point in my spiritual life. I went knowing that the Lord had accomplished something deep within me through my submission to His Word. And, I gained a better understanding of why it is important to be obedient to His will. As I went, I had an abiding sense of His presence resting upon me, beyond anything I had previously experienced.

This act of obedience carried me to the top of the riser and built a step *(platform)* upon which the Lord could intervene within my life. Then the Lord began to work upon this platform to accomplish all He desired to do within my being at this time. This visit became very special to me, for while there, I met the Lord in a wonderful way. From this man who deeply knew the Lord, I received an impartation that helped me tremendously in my ability to understand and respond to spiritual principles that would lead me to the Lord Himself.

Many times, when the Lord desires to use us, He will bring us through a test of obedience. This test may *(seemingly)* have nothing to do with the Lord's desire for us. But there will be a divinely arranged circumstance placed in our path which requires our obedience to Him. As we respond, we will encounter a very difficult cross with no possible detour around it. If we accept it, climb the riser and die to our desires, it will become a platform *(step)* upon which the Lord may do something which will be totally different, but very necessary. Our obedience will make a way for this to happen. It creates a platform that will become a "door" *("clefts of the rock"),* releasing the Lord to move in a higher realm involving us.

Some may wonder why the Lord is able to use "so and so" the way He does, but there is a reason. Unseen behind this activity is an open door of entrance into "the secret of the stairs" which they found and entered. This led them upward to the step *(platform)* that was created through their obedience, and upon which the Lord is doing mighty things in behalf of the one who has learned this secret of ascent on the stairs. This platform speaks of our being seated with Him in His Throne (Rev 3:21).

> "Then said Jesus unto His disciples, If any man will come after Me, let him deny himself, and take up his cross, and follow Me" Matt 16:24.

It is up to us. If we want to ascend, we must pay the price and begin to rise up, step upon step, together with Him.

> "Arise, My love, My fair one, and come away" SS 2:13b.

Chapter 6

The Approbation
Of God

"As the lily among thorns,
so is My love among the Daughters"
SS 2:2.

The Lord uses this highly contrasting and compelling imagery to emphasize His love for His Bride. This speaks of the "Approbation of God," or the fact of His singular attention and favor, which is uniquely toward her and rests upon her life. She has touched the heart of the Lord and He has become singularly interested in her. In the midst of others, she stands out before Him, as though she were the only one.

The most important compliment that we could possibly receive from the Lord would be to receive a similar expression of His approbation, concerning us. This would mean that we have become the recipient of His personal interest, concern, and activity. We have become His friend.

It is possible for each one of us to attract the attention of our Lord in such a way that He becomes interested in, and active within our life, as if we were the only person in the universe. This is a divine mystery that we cannot even begin to understand. However, it is very wonderful and rewarding to experience.

After the Lord had singled out the Bride from among the Daughters of Jerusalem by comparing her to a "lily among thorns," she told Him that He was as "the apple tree among the trees of the wood" SS 2:2a, 3a. Then she added,

> "I sat down **under His shadow** with great delight, and His fruit was sweet to my taste" SS 2:3b.

Notice that to her, His presence was but as a "shadow." She had not yet become interested in the reality of His personal presence. At this time, the center of her interest was in the things she desired to receive from Him, rather than in Him as a Person, and in seeking to personally know Him.

Thinking that all these gifts and blessings that He was able to supply would satisfy the hunger that was within her, she asked Him for even more:

> "Stay me with flagons, comfort me with apples" SS 2:5a.

He responded to this expression of her desire and gave her so much that she later said to Him,

> "I am sick of love" SS 2:5b.

After she had received from Him all that she wanted at that time, she told Him that He could leave and do as He pleased. Her only concern was where He would be, in case she had a need.

> "He feedeth among the lilies. Until the day break, and the shadows flee away, turn, my Beloved, and be Thou like a roe or a young hart upon the mountains of Bether" SS 2:16b-17.

At this time, her interest in the Lord centered around the things that she was able to get from Him. Thus, her testimony exposed her selfish attitude. The reason she

78

desired the Lord's involvement in her life was so He could provide for her wants. Therefore she said,

"My Beloved is mine" SS 2:16a.

If we listen carefully, our testimony will reveal the level of our spiritual growth and expose to us the desire, or intent of our heart in relation to the Lord.

Still, the Lord continued to bless her. Later, when He felt she was ready to go beyond her initial self-seeking, He began in a determined way to attract her attention away from all these things, and direct it to Himself. It is important that we notice the method He uses in doing this. While she was still very occupied within the "room" of her self-satisfaction, enjoying all of the gifts He had given her, He began to position Himself in ways that would provoke her to notice Him as a Person, apart from anything He could do for her.

"He standeth behind our wall, He looketh forth at the windows, shewing Himself through the lattice" SS 2:9b.

This "wall" speaks of the accumulative build-up of all those things which hinder, or separate us *(her)* from the Lord's presence. The materials that make up this hindering wall include, among other things, a lack in our spiritual perception, or understanding. This "spiritual dullness" is blinding her to all the possibilities in the realm of spiritual reality, into which the Bridegroom desires to lead her.

This wall greatly hinders her ability to perceive and experience the reality of cooperative communion with the Bridegroom. It is very important that we cultivate within us a spiritual sensitivity which will enable us to notice, and rightly respond to the Lord when He comes to take us further.

"Where there is no vision, the people perish" Prov 29:18a.

These "windows" represent her spiritual vision. She had experienced these "openings" through being quickened, or "touched" by His presence when she, from time to time, had momentarily recognized that there was "something more" *(the Lord Himself)* beyond all that she presently possessed. However, she had not yet fully responded to this "open door" into His presence. Therefore He remained without, seeking her attention through this window *(door)* that leads into His manifest presence. She was still indifferent to His desire to come within to be with her, because she had not experienced the lasting, inner satisfaction of intimate communion with Him.

The "lattice" speaks of the fact that His presence is always, in some measure, veiled. God is Spirit and can only be known through spiritual perception and recognition. Along with this, we cannot abide the full glory of His presence, until we come into the purity of life that is required for us to draw near to a holy and righteous God.

> "For what man knoweth the things of a man, save the spirit of man which is in him? even so the things of God knoweth no man, but the Spirit of God. Now we have received, not the spirit of the world, but the Spirit which is of God; that we might know the things that are freely given to us of God" 1 Cor 2:11-12.

The Heavenly Bridegroom, the Lord of all creation, stood alone, outside of all that He desired, patiently waiting for her to notice Him. He longed for her fellowship as He looked through the windows, gazing upon her in such a way that she could see His eyes. Finally, His patience met its reward. She saw Him and felt the intensity of His desire to be with her. All else faded as she responded to this, and invited Him to come into the "room" of her spiritual experience.

Immediately, He came within *(His manifest presence)* and began to teach her concerning the way of entrance into this new realm of spiritual life that He so desired for her. Then He invited her to come with Him into His chambers that she might begin to experience this new relationship of an abiding communion with Him.

> "Rise up, My love, My fair one, and come away" SS 2:10b.

His intention was to take her beyond the unsatisfying relationship she had maintained with Him, which was built upon her desire for all of the gifts and provisions that He had been giving her. As in the past, He desired to please and to satisfy her, but He had something far better to offer to her. Therefore, He waited until she noticed Him, and invited Him to come within. It was necessary that she recognize her need for Him alone. Only then would she be able to see her true spiritual condition and rightly respond to Him and to all He intended for her in becoming His Bride.

> "For, lo, the winter is past, the rain is over and gone; the flowers appear on the earth; the time of the singing of birds is come, and the voice of the turtle is heard in our land; the fig tree putteth forth her green figs, and the vines with the tender grape give a good smell" SS 2:11-13a.

The "winter" represents the time of spiritual barrenness she experienced while she was content with all of the blessings she had received, apart from the Lord Himself. The "rain" had showered all of these blessings upon her but is about to be removed from her. It is now "over and gone," as she enters the night season of her experience. It is here that she receives the treasures of darkness. The resultant "flowers" speak of the fruit of the spirit that develops as a result of her coming through this night season, and of being birthed into the realm of fellowship and identification with Him in His purposes.

The "voice of the turtle" speaks of her receiving a prophetic anointing that abides within her, and enables her to better express her love and worship to Him, as she comes into this new area of experience. The "fig tree" refers to Israel, and the "vine" to the Body of Christ. The present intense level of activity in each of these indicates that we are living in the last days of the Gentile age.

First, the Lord acknowledged her single eye toward Him.

> "O My dove, that art in the clefts of the rock, in the secret *places* of the stairs, let Me see thy countenance, let Me hear thy voice; for sweet is thy voice, and thy countenance is comely" SS 2:14.

Then, He expressed His love for her and told her how much He longed to hear the expression of her love toward Him, and how beautiful it sounded to Him. This is a divine mystery, that we could bring such joy and satisfaction to the Lord, Who has all of the hosts of heaven to enjoy.

After she had received and accepted these expressions of His love for her, she responded in thanksgiving and in worship. Then, He replied and told her that her voice was sweet. The Lord longs for us to personally express to Him our love for Him, and our desire to have His manifest presence abide with us. He greatly desires to hear our audible expression of worship toward Him.

Then, He placed her in the security of the "clefts of the rock" so her new-found, singular eye toward Him could be strengthened by expanding her personal knowledge of Him through a further revelation of His Person and glory.

> "O My dove, that art in the clefts of the rock, in the secret *places* of the stairs" SS 2:14a.

Now, she is in the place where He can begin to reveal to her the stairs, and the way of ascent upon them. Soon He will hear an even sweeter expression of thanksgiving and worship from her voice, as she begins to realize all that is happening to her, and how much better this is than her past, limited experience.

As these qualities developed within her being, He repeated to her the second time,

> "Arise, My love, My fair one, and come away" SS 2:13b.

He had shown her "the secret of the stairs" and the way to enter in. Now comes the problem that she, along with all of us, must face. He must wean her from the "bottle" (*"the winter is past, the rain is over and gone"*).

She had been more interested in His blessings (*"stay me with flagons, comfort me with apples"*), than she was in being with Him. She is still not willing to respond to His urgent call to "rise up" with Him, even though He has repeated it to her twice.

Therefore, He has no choice except to chasten her and further "tighten the rope," limiting her freedom to do as she pleases. There is only one way that this can be done. It must be done at "night," or in a time of spiritual darkness, when seemingly He withdraws the feeling of His presence, along with all of the blessings and things that He had given to her at her requests.

After He did this, we find her to be very upset.

> "By night on my bed I sought Him Whom my soul loveth: I sought Him, but I found Him not" SS 3:1.

The blessings are gone, and she is unable to find her way in the (seeming) spiritual darkness that has settled upon her. All at once, the methods that she once used to receive a spiritual blessing, along with the way the Lord used her in ministry, no longer worked. She was not able to feel, or sense the presence of the Lord, yet she discovered that she had never been so desirous for the Lord to reveal Himself to her as she was now.

Her reaction to the withdrawal of His presence and blessing was panic.

> "I will rise now, and go about the city in the streets, and in the broad ways I will seek Him Whom my soul loveth: I sought Him, but found Him not. The watchmen that go about the city found me: to whom I said, Saw ye Him Whom my soul loveth?" SS 3:2-3.

The watchmen are a type of the ministry. Before, she was content with all of the things she had received through them. Now, she is intensely hungry for the Lord Himself, and begins to look for Him. She said, "I will rise now, and go about the city." She sought Him in all the places where she had been previously blessed. She searched in vain, for she could not find Him.

She found a minister to whom she said, "Saw ye Him Whom my soul loveth?" However, the Lord did not permit this minister to help her, for the Lord was seeking to draw her to Himself. He desired to "sup with her" alone in His chambers, and also to renew her according to the potential that He had seen to be within her. Therefore, the only thing that this minister was able to say to her came from his own thoughts: "You are probably backsliding; you need to read your Bible and pray more."

In obedience, she read her Bible and prayed more as she had been told. But nothing happened, because the

Lord did not permit it to happen (*"The rain is over and gone"*). Therefore, she felt all the more as if the Lord had gone on a vacation, or had forsaken her. No matter to whom she spoke, or what advice they gave, none of these things worked or helped her in any way. The Lord had, insofar as feelings are concerned, withdrawn Himself from her.

In her distress, she sought for Him all the more. The intensity of this seeking, without seemingly receiving any results or satisfaction, caused her to cry out for the Lord Himself. Now, the very thing that the Lord has been waiting patiently for is beginning to form, deep within her. She is recognizing her need for Him, apart from things. She is desiring Him above all else. The "single eye" that the Lord had seen to be buried within her is beginning to surface and to focus.

She had prayed and said to the Lord,

> **"Tell me**, O Thou Whom my soul loveth, where **Thou feedest**, where Thou makest Thy flock to rest at noon: for why should I be as one that turneth aside by the flocks of Thy companions?" SS 1:7.

In the past, she had been satisfied with being nurtured only by others. Now she intensely desires the Lord to personally come that she might "sup with Him" (Rev 3:20). She is beginning to realize that only the Lord Himself is able to meet her need and has asked where she can find Him. The Lord heard this prayer and has begun, step upon step, to draw her to Himself.

It will greatly strengthen and encourage us in our seeking after the Lord Himself to understand the necessity of the Bride's going through this experience of "night." She had been content with the blessings that were readily available to her through an under-shepherd and had no desire to go further **until** the Lord removed these from her.

85

There is a time in our spiritual growth when we should begin to hear from the Lord Himself and receive directly from Him. We are to be "under tutors and governors **until** the time appointed of the Father" Gal 4:2. This "appointed time" had come for her. Therefore, even though she went to one watchman after another, she did not receive what she was seeking. Finally, in desperation, she turned to the Lord Himself, Who had been patiently waiting, but veiled behind the "lattice."

"It was but a little that I passed from them, but I found Him" SS 3:4a.

There had been a time when she was to receive from the Lord through others, but now the Lord caused their wells to dry up concerning her, as it was time for her to mature.

"I found Him" SS 3:4b.

He had been there all along, but now she saw Him in a different way. He is no longer the "shadow" that she had been accustomed to being near in the past. Now she clearly sees Him. During their renewed time of communion together, the Lord began to teach her concerning her ascent up the stairs into all that He had for her. Then, He waited for her to begin to climb toward Him, step upon step.

After she has submitted herself to this process and it has been personalized within her and tested, the Lord is able to say again to her, "rise up and come away," knowing that now she understands. She is ready to experience His approbation, or singular attention, and be further changed through times of personal intimate communion with Him alone. The shadow with which she had once been satisfied has become the Lord Himself.

We are not to attempt going on alone in our spiritual walk, apart from our pastor, or church fellowship. We would be as sheep that are led out amongst the wolves. The Lord has placed ministry in the Body of Christ for our good. The true purpose of ministry is to bring us to the Lord Himself. Thus, the proper outworking of this stage in our spiritual growth will result in the Lord being the center and circumference of our spiritual experience, having become our all in all. However, this should not take us away from our relationship to, and our need for, others in the Body of Christ.

This is the scriptural pattern, as given in Ephesians.

> "And He gave some, apostles; and some, prophets; and some, evangelists; and some, pastors and teachers . . . till we all come . . . unto a perfect *(mature)* man" Eph 4:11, 13a.

This "five-fold" ministry is given to bring us to the "cleft in the Rock," and to establish us there. As we rightly respond, in the right balance, to these ministries, a spiritual maturity will begin to develop, and the Lord Jesus Christ will become a personal reality within us. Only then will we be able to rise up and come away with Him.

> "It was but a little that I passed from them, but I found Him Whom my soul loveth" SS 3:4a.

Now, she has found the source of the satisfaction for which she had longed—the Lord Himself. She is ready, together with Him, to go further. Each time she comes up another step on the stairs to a new spiritual plateau, there is a further disclosure of "His ways" to her. These unfolding cycles of revelation and spiritual understanding will open to us, one upon another, as we respond to "the secret of the stairs," and begin to rise up, together with Him.

The Lord has led her through this period of darkness, in which it was very crucial that she not become discouraged and turn aside. She has been faithful, and has searched until she found Him.

> "I found Him Whom my soul loveth: I held Him, and would not let Him go" SS 3:4b.

She might have been turned aside by others, or become discouraged, but she had caught a glimpse of Him and could no longer be content, until she brought Him into her mother's house.

There, she became wonderfully satisfied, in the intimacy of His presence.

Chapter 7

Separated Unto Him

"I will rise now, and go about the city in the streets,
and in the broad ways I will seek Him
Whom my soul loveth:
I sought Him, but I found Him not"
SS 3:2.

The Lord had permitted the Bride to utterly fail in all of her efforts, as she sought for Him by attempting to recreate past experiences through which she had been blessed. Also, He caused all those to whom she went for help in finding Him, to be a complete disappointment to her.

"Saw ye Him Whom my soul loveth?" SS 3:3b.

Their inability to be of help added to her frustration. This desperation resulted in an enlarged capacity within her, which "made room" for the Lord to come further into her spiritual experience and bring a fuller revelation of Himself to her.

"It was but a little that I passed from them, but I found Him Whom my soul loveth: I held Him, and would not let Him go, until I had brought Him into my mother's house, and **into the chamber** of her that conceived me" SS 3:4.

Here is pictured, in the most intimate detail, the depth of personal closeness that can be experienced while in communion with our Heavenly Bridegroom.

Before this, she had been satisfied with the spiritual truth and blessings she was receiving through others. Because the Lord had something far better for her, He allowed her to become so dissatisfied with all she had known, that she began to seek Him alone.

The spiritual "hunger" that developed within her through this time of searching became so intense that she could find no satisfaction, apart from an experience of intimately, personally, "knowing" Him.

Notice that first, the "old" had to be removed so she would begin to seek the "new," which was far better. She had not realized this, and sought in desperation to recreate the old.

> "He taketh away the first, that He may establish the second" Heb 10:9b.

Our growth "unto the measure of the stature of the fulness of Christ" Eph 4:13b, includes our accepting and functioning in the gifts, ministries, and blessings that He is more than willing to share with us. These are a necessary "part" of the development of our spirituality, but we are not to abide there. As we continue to respond to His presence, and walk with Him in the outworking of His purposes, a growing sense of our identity with Him will develop within us.

Along with this, as we become more sensitive and perceptive in recognizing our Lord as the Divine Bridegroom Who is seeking our fellowship and love, and as we cultivate His abiding presence in our daily pattern of life, we will grow into increasing levels of spiritual maturity and experience.

The development of this two-fold relationship comes through "directive" communications from Him. This requires our becoming sensitive to His manifest presence. As we respond to Him in heart-obedience, we will gradually become more sensitive to His presence and learn how to move with Him in cooperative fellowship.

If we are sincere in our desire to come into the fullness of identification with Him in the outworking of His purposes, the time will come when He will begin to separate us from others, unto Himself. During this time we may be shut away from many Christian activities, that we might further develop a sensitivity to His Spirit and experience His manifest presence, daily. This requires our cultivating His anointing within our lives, for only as we develop a sensitivity to His voice and presence will we be enabled to respond to Him in obedience. It is during these times of personal visitation when we meet the Lord intimately, that we are changed by Him.

One of the most difficult areas in our spiritual progress is our being able to trust the faithfulness of the Lord, especially when we do not understand what He is doing within us, or in our circumstances. This inability to trust the Lord makes it very difficult for us to completely commit ourselves into His hands, and then abide there. Our lack of trust must be dealt with if we are to go further into the realm of spiritual life experience.

For example, the Lord once took me through a severe test involving the home we lived in. Our income had been cut off, and we were unable to pay the rent. The rental agency sent us a registered letter demanding us to be out of the house within a week, unless the rent was paid in full.

The time expired and even though we were informed that we would be moved into the street, I clearly felt the Lord saying we were not to leave. I prayed, "Lord, if You do not meet us soon, this will become the worst mess anyone has ever seen." It was an exceedingly impossible situation as there was absolutely no apparent way through. Again, the impression that we were not to move, but to continue trusting the Lord was strengthened within me, so, I obeyed. A short time later, the Lord, in a very unusual way, provided the rent and we were able to stay. Through this experience, I learned that His Word can be trusted and that He is faithful. I knew that I could trust my life in His hands.

Another experience helped me to come into a complete trust in His ability to care for us as a family. I had owned a TV cable system and understood electronic repair work. I felt quite limited as to my abilities in the ministry. Knowing I was responsible for my family, I decided if I were not successful in ministry, or if the Lord did not provide enough for us, I could go back into business and earn enough to support my family. So I purchased an expensive tube tester that was in a black alligator-like case, and put it in the attic of our cottage at the Bible School. Now, if it became necessary, I would get it down and use it to earn enough to cover our needs.

By having it available in the attic, I felt I had a reliable alternative. Then one day in class, the instructor began to talk about "little black alligators." He explained how these little creatures made the nicest pets. But, they needed to be fed each day, which meant they would grow. Then he added: "The problem is, the time will come when they will have become big enough to eat you."

Immediately, the Lord began to deal with me. I strongly felt that what had been presented about this alligator was intended for me. Later as I was waiting on the Lord, an unusual presence of the Lord came and He brought to my remembrance the tube tester I had put in the attic, "just in case." The Lord reminded me that it was in a black alligator case. He showed me that I was "feeding" it, because I was relying on it to meet our needs, rather than trusting Him implicitly.

Then He showed me that if I continued to rely upon this tube tester for security, it would begin to grow until it would devour me, concerning His will for my life. Now a battle started within me. I had paid a high price for "my alligator" and wanted to keep it. I complained to the Lord, "It cost all that money; what am I to do?"

A short time later, during a missionary convention, an urgent need was presented. The Lord began to deal with me to make a pledge and I resisted because I did not have the money to pay it. Then came the thought of the tube tester, and the Lord asked me if I was willing to give it up. In a few days, a postcard arrived from the man who had purchased my business. He needed a tube tester, had remembered that I had one, and wondered if I would be willing to sell it. I said yes, and was able to pay the missionary pledge I had made.

Sometimes the Lord presses us into a situation where it seems as if we are blindfolded with our hands tied behind our back, a gangplank before us, and a sword pressing into our back, telling us to walk off the end of it into nothingness. This "gangplank" is often a set of circumstances that has been arranged by the Lord to accomplish something specific within our lives. It may seem that as we walk off the end of the plank, it will be the end of everything. Yet in reality, He permits these things in order to show us His faithfulness, and to teach us to trust Him. If we are to become His Bride, then He must so work upon us that we learn to become dependent upon Him for everything.

The Lord has wonderfully proven Himself to me again and again. Each time I have seemingly walked off the end of this gangplank, I have landed right in His arms. These experiences have accomplished something deep within my being, beyond anything that could have been learned in any other way. I have seen the outworking of His redemption, and have experienced the reality and the faithfulness of my Heavenly Bridegroom. I have experientially learned that I can trust Him.

One of the greatest blessings we can ever receive is to experience the faithfulness of God. Sometimes we may be afraid, but the Lord will lead us to the place where we are able to place our implicit trust in Him and then rest. This is not easy, because this ability can only be wrought out through experience on the anvil of life. Yet, it may truly be said that if we are willing to completely entrust our lives to His hands, He will bring us through. We must recognize, however, that there is a difference between presumption and obedience. We must know that He is leading us.

Another experience which the Lord used to bring a correction in my walk with Him came while I was a student at Pinecrest during 1960. The Lord prompted me to set aside my weekly income check from the sale of my business for a purpose which He would make known later. I was being charged room and board for my family and tuition for classes; but now I did not have the money to pay these and my school bill began to climb. Before long, I was called into the office and asked for payment. I was not at liberty to reveal the reason I was unable to pay. I was then informed that I had to pay the past due amount within ten days or move out. The amount due now amounted to over $500. I had enough in the bank to pay this, yet the Lord had told me that I was to set this money aside.

A few days later, the Lord began to reveal to me many things about Abraham. He had told Abraham to go **up**

into the land that He would show him. When Abraham
arrived, there was a severe famine, yet the Lord had led
him there. Abraham, who had not yet experienced the
faithfulness of the Lord, left and went **down** into Egypt
for provision; but during his time there, he got into a lot
of trouble.

I saw that if Abraham had trusted the "word" he had
received from the Lord and stayed, the Lord would have
caused the very desert to spring up as a table of plenty.
The responsibility rested with the Lord because He had
told Abraham to go there. Therefore, during the time of
famine his need would have been met. But Abraham
turned to Egypt, a type of the world system, for provision.

The next day, I learned that a factory in town was
hiring, and if I would go in prepared for work, I could
start immediately. This seemed right, for I could then
approach the president of the school and tell him I was
working and would soon be able to pay the bill. The
Lord quickly reminded me of all He had just shown me
about Abraham. Now I realized that I was about to go to
"Egypt" to have my needs met, rather than trust Him.
It was not easy to say no. But I had no choice if I was to
please the Lord and truly learn to trust Him. I had to
wait for His provision.

There were only three days remaining until I would
be told to leave. While I was on a ladder, patching the
plaster on a ceiling, the following thoughts ran through
my mind. I said within myself, "In the past when the
Lord spoke to me, He always made a way through for
me. This is the same voice telling me to set this money
aside. If this is truly the Lord, He will make a way. If
not, I need to know. So, I will get down from this ladder,
go and tell the school president that I cannot pay the
bill. Then, I will go to my apartment, pack and leave. 'I
do not understand, Lord, but I will find a place to live
and I will serve You anyway.'"

After I had made this determination, a very heavy presence of the Lord came upon me; so much so, that I had to bend over the top of the ladder to keep from falling off. The Lord spoke again and said, "This is what I wanted to hear. Now, go and use the money to pay your school bill." I was very disappointed, as I wanted to go to the president of the school and tell him that I could not pay. I thought that perhaps something spectacular would happen when I did. However, I very reluctantly withdrew the money from the bank and paid the school the amount due.

About two weeks later, I received further understanding concerning Abraham. The Lord showed me that He had miraculously given Abraham a son, Isaac, who was the result of the promise that had been given to Abraham and Sarah. Because of the impossible circumstances and the greatness of this miracle, Abraham now loved Isaac more than the Lord, and a correction became necessary.

Likewise, the Lord showed me that I too had received a promise. My promise *(Isaac)* was Pinecrest. This had previously been given to me through a very clear and unusual visitation from the Lord. While waiting upon the Lord, I had been caught up and completely engulfed in a visible Glory, which I saw in brilliant color.

The Lord had made known to me—without my seeing any form or hearing any words, but rather through an understanding that came into me through this moving, visible, Glory—that I was to establish a school at Pinecrest which would emphasize His anointing and manifest presence. Also, I was to teach His ways, and prepare many for His visitation and last-day intervention purposes.

After learning of His purpose for me, "my ministry" began to mean more to me than my times of fellowship with the Lord. I had become so involved with how this vision could come into being, that the Lord had to deal with me to draw me back to Himself. My seeking the ministry that He had for me began to occupy so much of my time and energy, that I left the place of an abiding communion with the Lord, which I had once known.

Then I realized that the Lord could not allow me to go on this way. He said, "You love your Isaac *(Pinecrest)* more than Me. Therefore, I led you up on the mount (I was on top of a ladder when all this happened) with Isaac *(Pinecrest)*, to offer him. Then you raised the knife by saying, 'I will tell the president of the school that I cannot pay the bill, and I will pack, leave, and serve You anyway.' When I saw that you were ready to slay Pinecrest in obedience, I was then satisfied."

Once again, the Lord was first in my life; a correction had been made. This was all that the Lord wanted of Abraham. When Abraham raised the knife, Isaac immediately became second in Abraham's life. He had restored the first place in his life to the Lord, and the Lord was satisfied. Immediately, a substitute sacrifice was provided.

At this present time, the vision which I received from the Lord has come into being. I am the president of a Bible School at Pinecrest, as He had revealed. Now, I can honestly say that it is not mine; it belongs to the Lord, for "Isaac" has been given back to Him. I can truly trust the faithfulness of the Lord to accomplish His purposes in my life and in Pinecrest, whatever the circumstances may be.

The Lord desires to work out His creative purpose in each of our lives, even though it may seem to lead to death. The way into this new experience of life is by taking up our cross and following Him. Jesus said, "Except a corn of wheat fall into the ground and die, it abideth alone: but if it die, it bringeth forth much fruit" John 12:24b. He will abide faithful in all. This has been made experientially real to me many times. I could have gone to work and paid my school bill, but the loss would have been eternal.

The Lord may allow circumstances in our lives that appear impossible in order to reveal His faithfulness to us. Then He will be able to bring us to the place where we can, in loving trust, submit to and become dependent upon Him. As we are His Bride, He has a right to expect this of us. This is why the Bride said, "Draw me, we **will run** after Thee." "To run" suggests a reckless daring, whereby we trust Him in spite of circumstances, rather than because of them. No longer are our responsibilities or needs to be a hindrance to our obedience to Him. So often we miss the Lord at this point.

A young man, who was called to serve the Lord, had a very good position and the Lord began to lead him to relocate. He learned that his company was willing to transfer him to a branch office in the place where he was being led to go. He said, "I will not go unless they pay me more than I make now." I felt the grieving of the Holy Spirit when I heard this. He had not learned to be obedient to the leading of the Lord, nor to trust His faithfulness.

The Lord does not accept us on the basis of our terms. The Scripture says, "For many are called, but few are chosen" Matt 22:14. Or, "Many are called, but few are willing to pay the price in order to be chosen." Our being chosen is always based on our obedience in qualifying. This is why the Lord said, "**If any man** will come after Me, let him deny himself, and take up his cross and follow Me" Matt 16:24b. Notice that the Lord said "If." It is up to us to obey.

Through the progressive decisions we make in choosing His ways, and by our diligently cultivating our relationship with Him, His image and likeness becomes fashioned within our being. This is better understood through the following example. Tickets to enter the Smithsonian Institute were given to two men. Each knew that he was to go at an appointed time. The first man continued to rejoice over the fact that He had a ticket to get in and this was all that he did. But the second man began to read and study about the things that were there. He spent all his time in preparation for this trip, so he could get the most out of it. The day came that they arrived, and presented their tickets. Then, they came to what appeared to be a large rock. To the first, it had no value or purpose. But to the second it spoke volumes, because he had studied and understood why it was there. There had been an inner preparation in his life which gave it meaning.

Sometimes we sing about having a mansion "just over the hill top" and speak about the "streets of gold." But unless there is something within us that gives meaning to His call for us to be seated together with Him in His throne, and unless we have come into His chambers for times of communion with Him, then all this will only be as that "stone" was to the first man. It will have no meaning or apparent value.

"By **night** on my bed I sought Him" SS 3:1a.

He leads us through these dark places; but afterward, when the light breaks, we discover that we have a new understanding of God. While I was going through my experience on top of the ladder, the true purpose of Abraham's experience never occurred to me. It was later, while waiting on the Lord, that it came before me. Then I understood the experience I had gone through. This gave me a deeper confidence in the Lord,

99

and built something into the very fiber of my being that strengthened me.

Now I was more willing, in obedience to Him, to take a step beyond that which seemed to be reasonable; for I knew I could trust the Lord in whatever situation He would bring my way. As the Lord begins to build this confidence in our lives, He separates us from the "many" *(the Daughters of Jerusalem)* and begins to view us as His "singular" Bride.

Only then He will be able to say to us, "O My dove, that art in the clefts of the rock, in the secret *places* of the stairs" SS 2:14a. Here we can rest in the approbation of His favor, and the security of His protection.

The Bride had just revealed her spiritual condition through her first confession, "My Beloved is mine" SS 2:16a. Now, the Lord is ready to begin the process of separation that will bring her into the place where He will become first in her life and interest. Then she will be able to trust Him with her care and protection.

To accomplish this, He brought her into the wilderness for a time. This wilderness was a place of barrenness and desolation, where she seemingly was separated from all the things which meant so much to her. During this time of separation, these things began to lose their value, and became as nothing.

> "By night on my bed I sought Him Whom my soul loveth: I sought Him, but I found Him not" SS 3:1.

She had come to the end of her own abilities, and confessed her loss.

In the barrenness of this wilderness experience, He brought forth to her, a very special revelation of Himself.

"Who is this that cometh out of the wilderness like
pillars of smoke, perfumed with myrrh and frankincense, with all powders of the merchant? Behold His
bed . . . threescore valiant men are about it" SS 3:6-7a.

She marveled at this display of His power and might.
Now she began to realize the ability of the Lord to care
for her and bring her through to the fullness of everything He had intended for her.

In this wilderness setting, He revealed Himself to her
in all of His Glory and might. Now she saw Jesus only;
all other things had lost their value, and she began to
fall in love with Him alone. Also, carefully notice that
He had been in the wilderness with her, the entire time.

"Until the day break, and the shadows flee away, I
will get Me to the mountain of myrrh, and to the hill
of frankincense. Thou art all fair, My love; there is no
spot in thee" SS 4:6-7.

Now the Lord is beginning to deal with the Bride in
this further step of separation. There is, in our spiritual
experience, a continuing, progressive unfolding of our
identification with the Lord as a member of His Body
and as His potential Bride. First, He must establish us on
the Rock, the Lord Jesus Christ, Who is the foundation
of our experience in salvation. Judicially, or legally,
through the redemption that Jesus wrought in our
behalf on the cross, the Lord sees us as perfect through
the blood of Jesus. He can truly say to us, "there is no
spot in thee." We must believe this, and fully accept it
before He will be able to take us any further.

Therefore, He tells the Bride,

"Thou art all fair, My love; there is no spot in thee" SS
4:7.

He assures her that He sees her through His blood
that was shed upon the cross in her behalf. We also

101

have this assurance because forgiveness, cleansing, and purification are gifts. We cannot earn these, but simply believe that Jesus died on the cross in our behalf and accept them by faith. Then, as we walk with Him, what He sees us to be, begins to become a reality in our lives. This is the miracle of redemption. We believe, and then we become.

After He told her that she was "all fair" in His sight, He said,

> "Come with Me from Lebanon, My spouse, with Me from Lebanon: look from the top of Amana, from the top of Shenir and Hermon, from the lions' dens, from the mountains of the leopards" SS 4:8.

He is appealing for her to leave all the places in her past life that have hindered her spiritual growth, and which pose a danger to her developing sensitivity to His presence, and to her abiding fellowship with Him.

This process of sanctification will determine how far we will be able to go with Him. In love, He will call us away from the borders of worldly things, with all their enticements.

"Come with Me **from** . . ." SS 4:8a.

He will say this to each one of us, if truly our desire is to "run after Him."

Chapter 8

A Time For Being Shut Away

"A garden inclosed is My sister, My spouse;
a spring shut up, a fountain sealed.
Thy plants are an orchard of pomegranates,
with pleasant fruits; camphire, with spikenard,
spikenard and saffron; calamus and cinnamon,
with all trees of frankincense; myrrh and aloes,
with all the chief spices"
SS 4:12-14.

Her first testimony had been, "My Beloved is mine" SS 2:16a. The Lord accepted this, and allowed the Bride to have all of the things she desired. At the same time, He began to draw her to Himself by causing her to notice His interest in her.

"He standeth behind our wall, He looketh forth at the windows, shewing Himself through the lattice" SS 2:9b.

As she noticed Him looking through the window, longing to be invited into the room of her spiritual life, there was within her a deep inner stirring toward Him.

Now she began to desire Him, rather than all the things she had once wanted. He acknowledged her "single eye" which was beginning to see Him alone, and

103

in a penetrating expression of love, He said to her, "O My dove" SS 2:14a. Because of this single eye, He could begin to inwardly change her into the Bride He desired her to be.

In her first confession she had said,

> "My mother's children were angry with me; **they** made me the keeper of the vineyards; but mine own vineyard have I not kept" SS 1:6b.

She had been a very dedicated worker for the Lord. Even in the heat of the day, while others rested, she worked until she became burned by the sun, *("I am black, but comely" SS 1:5a)*. During this time, she did not personally know the Lord, neither did she know His voice nor His leadings. She did only as others told her to do *("they made me the keeper of the vineyards")*.

She had been so faithful in doing all that was required of her, that her own vineyard had been neglected. This neglected vineyard speaks of the "ground" upon which the Lord comes in order to work within our lives. It encompasses the people and the circumstances which the Lord uses to bring about our spiritual development and growth (Eph 2:10). It becomes "good ground" Matt 13:8b, when we place the Lord in full control of our lives.

The special places that we have "sanctified," or set apart for our times of fellowship with the Lord have much to do with the quality of the atmosphere within this neglected vineyard. We should make the total area of our life experience as an "open door" for the Lord to enter. It is this which encourages and releases the Lord to become active in making of us the Bride He desires.

He will always continue to use us to minister to and meet the needs of others. However, our times of communion with Him are more important to Him than anything that we could do for Him. He is to have first place in our lives.

> "Come, My beloved, **let us** go forth into the field; **let us** lodge in the villages. **Let us** get up early to the vineyards; **let us** see if the vine flourish, whether the tender grape appear, and the pomegranates bud forth: **there** will I give thee My loves" SS 7:11-12.

It is not that one is more important than the other. Rather, our ministry will be much more effective and productive when it is the result of, and flows out from, our times of communion with Him.

Most servants of the Lord who fail or get into serious problems, do so because of negligence at this very point. They work so hard for the Lord that they become spiritually weakened and succumb to temptation. This happened to the Bride. Thus, she confessed, "My mother's children were angry with me." It is crucial that we maintain quality times of meditative scripture reading, prayer, and waiting upon the Lord. She had neglected her own spiritual development and growth, along with her times of communion with the Lord, through working diligently for Him. We must keep in mind that our ability to give can only come from that which we have within us to give.

We are called to work with the Lord, rather than for Him.

> "And He goeth up into a mountain, and calleth unto Him whom He would: and they came unto Him. And He ordained twelve, **that they should be with Him**, and that He might send them forth to preach" Mark 3:13-14.

If we are faithful in our part, which is "being with Him," then He will be faithful in His part, to "send us forth."

She had asked the Lord to "stay me with flagons, comfort me with apples" SS 2:5a. In response to her desire, He brought her to the banqueting table and blessed her so abundantly with all she wanted, that she became filled beyond the capacity she had at that time.

"For I am sick of love" SS 2:5b.

We are to enjoy the blessings, and use to the fullest all of the gifts that the Lord has given. Yet these are not meant to be our goal. Rather, they are to be the means of meeting the needs of others, and of enlarging our capacity and our desire for Him.

Outwardly, she seemed to be satisfied and content. However, the Lord knew that inwardly, she could not continue to be satisfied and fulfilled by just having these things. She had seen Him, and was moved deep within her being toward Him. Now, He was ready to show her that there was something better for her, beyond all these things that He was able to give her.

To accomplish this, He allowed her to enter into, or experience, a time of spiritual darkness.

"**By night** on my bed I sought Him Whom my soul loveth" SS 3:1a.

During this time of darkness, all spiritual things seemed to become elusive or obscure. She realized the emptiness of the possession of things alone, and frantically began to search for Him.

"I will rise now, and go about the city in the streets, and in the broad ways I will seek Him" SS 3:2a.

During this time of searching, she began to understand how incomplete she had been without Him. By the time she found Him, a real change had taken place within her. She was now able to say:

"It was but a little that I passed from them *(all of the things that she once sought after)*, but I found Him Whom my soul loveth: I held Him, and would not let Him go" SS 3:4a.

The Lord expresses this same spiritual principle to the Laodicean church.

"Because thou sayest, **I am rich**, and increased with goods, **and have need of nothing**; and knowest not that thou art wretched, and miserable, and poor, and blind, and naked: I counsel thee to buy of Me gold tried in the fire, that thou mayest be rich" Rev 3:17-18a.

The Laodiceans sought after and were satisfied with possessions. Therefore, the Lord called attention to their true need: "gold tried in the fire." Gold speaks of the divine nature, His image and likeness being wrought out within our being. We become like Him, as we spend much time with Him.

Now He is ready to take her a step further. In order to make a deep and lasting impression within her concerning Himself, He brought before her a glorious revelation of His Person and presence as He came forth from the wilderness, clothed in all of His manifest glory and sovereign power.

"Who is this that cometh **out of the wilderness** like pillars of smoke, perfumed with myrrh and frankincense, with all powders of the merchant? Behold His bed, which is Solomon's; threescore valiant men are about it, of the valiant of Israel" SS 3:6-7.

Through this experience, she realized her need for Him, and felt the comfort and the security of being with Him. She saw the portrayal of His love for her, along with the display of His ability to protect her and bring her through even the most difficult of situations.

Immediately after the excitement and glory of this experience, the Lord made an arrangement where she became as "a garden inclosed" SS 4:12a. Here, she was separated for a time from material influences and outside activities, unto the Lord Himself. During this time of separation within the Garden, all that she had come to know about the Lord will become personalized *(made personally real)* within her spiritual experience. Then, in His time and place, that which she has become while within the Garden will find its full expression and outworking through her daily life experiences. She is about to experience what the Lord meant when He said,

"Buy of Me gold tried in the fire" Rev 3:18b.

This "Garden inclosed" was designed to bring forth the very best from the potential that the Lord had seen to be within her. It was situated in a very beautiful setting. However, it represented a realm of intense "personal dealings," so she hesitated in entering. The Lord knew she would attempt to leave before He could accomplish all He desired within her. He therefore built a high wall around the Garden, making it completely enclosed so she would not be able to leave. The Lord is able to keep us where He has placed us.

This high wall also hindered all, except the Lord, from entering. It separated her from the fellowship of her friends, and from those who would attempt to occupy her time. Also, during this set-apart time, her gifts seemingly failed to operate, and her "ministry" was cut off. Now, she was separated from all of the people and things which she had become accustomed to and dependent upon in her spiritual life. She became as a "Garden inclosed," separated unto the Lord Himself.

The nine plants (SS 4:13-14) that are mentioned as

being in this Garden are types of the nine-fold fruit of the Spirit. These represent the "quality" of life which is beginning to develop and become manifest within her, during this time of separation. The Garden in bloom speaks of the spiritual maturity now unfolding within her, a beautiful display of righteousness, peace, and joy, as she grows in spiritual understanding and wisdom. During this time of being set apart, there was often a desire within her for expression, or ministry: "If I could just get out and share this." But the Lord had made her a "Garden inclosed."

Through being shut in by the Lord for a season, she became more sensitive in her ability to recognize His presence, and was able to respond more promptly to His desire for her fellowship. We were created for His pleasure (Rev 4:11). There are times when the Lord desires to be personally alone with us, that He might sup with us, and then we with Him (Rev 3:20). This will lead us into the experience of the "fellowship of His sufferings" Phil 3:10b, as He shares His burdens with us.

There are other areas of separation. There are those who are called to a ministry of intercession. Being an intercessor requires much more from us than our times of prayer. It involves our becoming identified with the problem, or need, in order to pray it through. Intercession is born of the Spirit and operates through inner travail. It means getting alone and wrestling with a burden until it is brought to birth through the agony of birth pains. A ministry of intercession is effectual and is worked out in the prayer closet, alone with the Lord. There are those who are called to this hidden ministry of intercession who are not known to man, but known only to the Lord, and have become as a "Garden inclosed" to Him.

There are others who are shut in with the Lord in hidden ministries, who have a part in bringing to birth many lives. Some of these had a part in the forming of my spiritual life. During times when I was going through some very intense struggles, through the agony of their intercession and prayers, God was able to accomplish something special within me. Without them, I could not be where I am today. There is great responsibility and reward in a hidden ministry of this type. The Lord is looking to and fro across the earth for someone to "stand in the gap"; someone who will stand between the need and the Lord, and then travail until the Lord is able to move upon the situation and accomplish His purpose.

There are those whom the Lord leads into this "Garden inclosed" to remain there. Some of the Lord's choicest saints are separated from the world and enclosed within this Garden, that He might come to them as He wills, to enjoy times of fellowship and communion. The extravagance that the Lord expressed in His creation is evident to us, which we all enjoy as we witness the manifold and multi-colored flowers of spring, and then the rich brilliance of color in the departing leaves of fall. So also, He can afford the luxury of being extravagant in setting aside "whom He will" for His purpose and glory. Thus, within this "Garden inclosed" are those who are so completely given to Him that they are known to Him alone.

There are still others whom the Lord draws into this Garden to stay for only a limited time. He leads these back out again to become a witness of all they received while there alone in the Garden with Him Whom they love. Those who desire more of the Lord, but are not yet ready to be drawn into this Garden experience, will be able to pick fruit from the lives of these who had been within, until they also desire to come within this "Garden inclosed."

When the Lord came into the Garden to be with His Bride—as He had entered the Garden of old "in the cool of the day *(evening)*" Gen 3:8, to walk with Adam—she experienced the peace and the joy that results from being in His presence. As she basked in the warmth of this presence, she prayed that the wind *(the Holy Spirit)* would come and blow upon her Garden. She desired this new inward beauty that was developing within her to become as a beautiful fragrance that would flow out from her being, and bless Him.

> "Awake, O north wind; and come, thou south; blow upon my garden, that the spices thereof may flow out" SS 4:16a.

This "wind" is a type of the Holy Spirit. When Nicodemus came to Jesus, the Lord dealt with him about entering the Kingdom of God. Nicodemus asked if this was comparable to re-entering the womb. Jesus responded by likening it to the wind. He said, "The wind bloweth where it listeth, and thou hearest the sound thereof, but canst not tell whence it cometh, and whither it goeth"; then He added, "so is every one that is born of the Spirit" John 3:8.

The north wind represents chastening, or correction; the south wind speaks of edification and blessing. This two-fold working of the wind brings, first, correction to our spiritual walk, either through or along with teaching; and then, secondly, blessing and edification. The desire of the Lord is to bring us through as painlessly as possible.

When the Bride prayed, "Awake, O north wind," she was giving the Holy Spirit permission to bring about these needed changes within her life that she might be in alignment with His purposes. Whatever the cost might be, she desired to flow in harmony with Him. His chastening hand upon our lives is truly a great blessing when we understand the purpose for it, and feel His love as it is applied.

"For whom the Lord loveth He chasteneth" Heb 12:6a.

As the Holy Spirit worked within her in answer to her prayer giving Him permission to chasten her, she began to notice the changes that were taking place within her being. Now she understood that the purpose of the "north wind" was to change her, that she might become a Bride that would truly please the Lord. This caused thanksgiving and worship to rise up within her, and flow out to Him. Now, she was able to ask with confidence, His correcting hand upon her life.

"Come, thou south; blow upon my garden, that the spices thereof may flow out. Let my Beloved come into His garden, and eat His pleasant fruits" SS 4:16b.

As she felt the warmth and comfort of the south wind, she was able to enter a place of rest in His presence, knowing He would do what was right in her behalf and that her response was pleasing to Him.

There is a "lifting" quality to the presence of the Lord. As we respond to His presence, we will begin to flow with it, as being lifted by the wind. As we continue to wait in His presence, we will be quickened by the Holy Spirit and empowered, or enabled to move with Him as He leads. As this takes place, it will be confirmed to us through a further unfolding and understanding of His Word, which will cause us to more deeply trust and love Him. It is important to understand that all spiritual experiences must agree with the written Word of God.

As these north and south winds each had their effect upon her, and accomplished their purposes within her, she cried out,

"Let my Beloved come into His garden, and eat His pleasant fruits" SS 4:16b.

He quickly responded to this and said,

"I am come into My garden" SS 5:1a.

This speaks of His "manifest presence." The Lord is omnipresent; that is, He is everywhere. He fills heaven and earth (see Jer 23:24). But the manifest presence of the Lord is something more than this. The word "manifest" means that His presence becomes localized, and is made consciously apparent to one or more of our five senses.

Through His omnipresence we are made aware of the sovereign power of God and receive a sense of Divine presence. However, through His manifest presence, He comes to us in such a way that we not only sense His nearness, but also are made consciously aware of His Person and personality. This brings us into an awareness and knowledge of His mind and His feelings. Jesus said,

"If any man hear My voice, and open the **door** *(the point of transition from His omnipresence into His manifest presence)*, I will come in to him, and will sup with him, and he with Me" Rev 3:20b.

"Supping," in the oriental sense, means an intimate, personal exchange. Thus, the Lord comes to us in this intimate and personal way to share His personality and thoughts with us.

"**I am come** into My garden, My sister, My spouse: **I have gathered** My myrrh with My spice; **I have eaten** My honeycomb with My honey" SS 5:1a.

Then He adds,

"Eat, O friends; drink, yea, drink abundantly, O beloved" SS 5:1c.

Notice the exchange, "Drink abundantly, O beloved"

113

then, "Eat, O friends." Paul understood this principle and applied it to his ministry. He said,

> "For we which live are alway delivered unto death for Jesus' sake, that the life also of Jesus might be made manifest in our mortal flesh. So then death worketh in us, but life in you" 2 Cor 4:11-12.

Paul ministered his very life to others. All true ministry includes the giving of the spiritual substance of the minister's life along with the Word that he ministers. Many come to feed upon the lives of those who have this quality of spiritual substance within them, and then go away leaving them drained. This is especially true of those who are heavily anointed. Ministry works death in the one who is giving, but life in all who receive. Jesus said,

> "Except ye eat the flesh of the Son of man, and drink His blood, ye have no life in you" John 6:53b.

After a time of giving out in ministry, we must come back to the Source of all life, our Lord Jesus Christ and partake again of His life, in order to regain that which has been given out to others.

The Lord comes to fellowship with us, and also to change us and strengthen us while we are alone with Him in this "Garden inclosed." Then He shares us with others, who presently are not able to come into this place of intimate communion with Him. We feed on Him, then others may come and feed on us, and thereby receive His life through us. This places a great responsibility upon each of us, that the true source of our life be Jesus. Others must not be drawn to us, but directed to Jesus.

As others partake of our spiritual life and experiences, a spiritual hunger will be created within them. As this partaking continues, these will begin to become discontented, and will realize there is something better than continuing to be satisfied with feeding on the experiences of another. Thus, they will begin to look for the Lord Himself. Now, they will be able to say to the Lord, as we once did,

> "Tell me, O Thou Whom my soul loveth, where Thou feedest, where Thou makest Thy flock to rest at noon: for why should I be as one that turneth aside by the flocks of Thy companions?" SS 1:7.

The Lord answered and said,

> "If thou know not . . . go thy way forth by the footsteps of the flock" SS 1:8a.

It is very important, at this point, that we ourselves know the way and are able to lead these to the Lord Himself.

Many will be enabled to come into a greater experience in the reality of the Lord Jesus Christ, and into a personal relationship with Him because we have been spending time with Jesus, and have learned to sup with Him. Through our times of communion and prayer, as we continue to sup with Him, we receive much spiritual substance into our being. Now, He will allow others to come and feed on us, as we feed on Him.

> "Eat, O friends; drink, yea, drink abundantly" SS 5:1c.

Notice that the Lord gladly tells others that they can come and feed on our spiritual life and experience.

There is a tremendous need in our day for those who have a quality relationship with the Lord, and have spiritual substance within their lives. These, in turn, will be able to feed others, whose spiritual hunger has not found a place of satisfaction.

115

Chapter 9

Shut In
With Him Alone

"A garden inclosed is My sister, My spouse;
a spring shut up, a fountain sealed"
SS 4:12.

The Bride has come to the place in her spiritual experience where she is able to view the Bridegroom with a single eye and respond to Him as He desires. She has progressed in her relationship with Him to the extent that she is no longer content with spiritual gifts and blessings, apart from His presence. She intensely desires to be with the Lord in the outworking of His purposes, whatever they may be, or wherever they may lead.

To bring about this change within her, the Lord prepared a special "Garden inclosed" in which she became as a "spring shut up, a fountain sealed." Here, she was alone, separated from all that she had known in her past experiences. Her spiritual gifts and abilities seemingly dried up causing her to feel spiritually dead. Now she has become very conscious of her spiritual need.

At this very critical moment in her spiritual experience, while she was feeling this intense inner need, the Lord came within the Garden and revealed Himself to her as a Bridegroom Who greatly desires to be with His Bride. During this time, she experienced a very beautiful and satisfying time of fellowship with Him alone. She discovered that she enjoyed His presence much more than in the past, when her preoccupation had been solely spent in seeking the blessings and gifts He was able to give. Now she had found that she wanted to be with Him. She became very sensitive to His feelings and desires.

This "Garden inclosed" is a special atmosphere that is created by a Divine arrangement for those who have come to the place in their spiritual experience where they desire Him above all else. Our abiding within this "Garden inclosed" allows the Lord to develop the pattern of His activity in our behalf as He establishes us in this environment of His rest. We are to wait upon the Lord within the confines of this Garden and allow Him to bring forth the spiritual qualities that He sees to be within us.

Those who truly love the Lord will actively seek to cultivate His abiding presence. This causes the Lord to become singularly interested in them. Then, He will create deep within each, an intense spiritual hunger. This inner heart cry will find its expression as a prayer, "Draw me," which He longs to answer. This will result in our becoming able to make an unqualified commitment to Him, "we will run after Thee." These together culminate in a very beautiful and satisfying "Garden" experience, of which we can testify, "The King hath brought me into His chambers" SS 1:4a.

He has a Garden, or a "prepared place" for each one of us who will sincerely pray this prayer. As we obediently respond to the spiritual hunger that He has placed within us, and begin to "run" after Him, He will reveal to us the secret of climbing the stairs that lead upward into the experience of His abiding presence.

While she was experiencing the "joy unspeakable" of being alone with Him in the Garden, she asked for the Holy Spirit to come to her and quicken her, that her life might more fully become a blessing to her heavenly Bridegroom, the Lord Jesus Christ.

> "Awake, O north wind; and come, thou south; blow upon my garden, that the spices thereof may flow out" SS 4:16a.

This prayer, "Awake, O north wind," is crucial to those who desire something more than their present spiritual experience. It is our invitation to the Holy Spirit to become active within us, to develop the quality and the beauty that will please the Lord, and along with this, enable us to become a "witness" to others. This is the fruit, or the satisfying reward, that comes as a result of our yielding to His working within us.

Her second request in this prayer, "Come, thou south; blow upon my garden" also has a very special part in the outworking of our spiritual experience. This speaks of the Holy Spirit quickening us so the spiritual beauty that has been developing within us will begin to flow out of our being to bring satisfaction and pleasure to our Heavenly Bridegroom. As He receives this expression of our love, it will also be witnessed by others, and we become to them a "taste" of the satisfying love-relationship that is developing between us and the Bridegroom, which will stir them to seek Him also.

Only as we have unconditionally submitted our will and all our circumstances to the power of the Holy Spirit, and allow Him to freely work within us to accomplish all that He desires, only then can this prayer for the "south wind" to blow upon our Garden find its full outworking and expression within our lives. This

119

prayer will result in an abiding anointing *(the south wind)* that will bring forth from within us all the beauty of our Heavenly Bridegroom, and enable us to be more fully available to Him.

> "Let my Beloved come into His garden, and eat His pleasant fruits" SS 4:16b.

The changes which have taken place within her—from self-centered "getting" to Christ-centered "giving" —so please her that she now invites the Lord to abide in the very center of her being for His own satisfaction and purposes. This is a complete reversal from her past desires and requests which concerned only the gifts and blessings He had to give.

Now, she greatly desires that her life might provide some pleasure and satisfaction to the Lord and she longs to be with Him. No longer is she satisfied with only being a "keeper of the vineyards" SS 1:6b, for the benefit of her mother's children. She feels free to ask where she can find His chambers, so she can be with Him.

> "Tell me, O Thou Whom my soul loveth, where Thou feedest" SS 1:7a.

He had been patiently waiting to hear this and quickly responded,

> "I am come into My garden, My sister, My spouse: I have gathered My myrrh with My spice; I have eaten My honeycomb with My honey; I have drunk My wine with My milk" SS 5:1a.

During this time of quiet fellowship with her in the Garden, the Lord found many things within her life that pleased and satisfied Him.

The Lord greatly desires to come and fellowship with us. This is a mystery that we are little able to comprehend. Nevertheless, He truly experiences satisfaction and joy during His times of fellowship and communion with us. When the Lord created man, He placed within human nature a profound capacity for man's compatibility with Him (Gen 1:27). Therefore, He created within us the desire and the ability to respond to His presence, and then established within our pattern of daily life the possibility of an environment that would make room for the fulfillment of His desire to commune and fellowship with us.

The first picture that we are given of the outworking of this created capacity which the Lord placed within us is seen in the Garden of Eden. The Lord came at specific times, in the "cool of the evening," and walked with Adam in the Garden. He has placed within the pattern of each of our lives a "cool of the evening." There is within each one of us a unique time when we can best meet the Lord. For some, it is early in the morning. Others can best commune with the Lord late in the evening. It is very important that we seek out and identify this special time, and set it apart for our times of fellowship with the Lord. He will quickly respond to our desire to walk with Him, as He walked with Adam: "I am come into My garden, My sister, My spouse."

First, there was her step of obedience in being willing to be shut away from everything to which she had become accustomed in her past experience, and to become as a "Garden inclosed" unto Him. During this time of being separated unto Him alone in the Garden, she had been so completely changed that now she longed for Him alone. Her eye had truly become single toward Him.

The "Garden inclosed" that she became had now become His Garden. In anticipation of His times of

121

communion with her, He is able to say with an expression of joy,

"I am come into **My Garden**, My sister, My spouse"
SS 5:1a.

Now His approbation, or singular love was resting upon her life and she has become attentive to it. He may freely come to her, and commune with her in His chambers or walk through the vineyards with her in the outworking of His purposes, as He pleases.

Chapter 10

The Test Of Obedience

"Behold, I stand at the door, and knock:
if any man hear My voice, and open the door,
I will come in to him,
and will sup with him, and he with Me"
Rev 3:20.

The fact that the Lord will come to us and knock on the door of our heart is certain. He may come, however, at a time that is not convenient for us. Nevertheless, He expects a prompt, unquestioning response from us.

The word "If" in the above verse tells us that the Lord's coming into the "room" of our spiritual life is conditional. It indicates that we have been given the option either to ignore His approaches, or to invite Him to come within. Our prompt obedience in response to His knocking, even when it takes place at a time that is inconvenient, will bring us, together with Him, through the door of entrance into His manifest presence.

"I love them that love Me; and those that seek Me early *(respond promptly)* shall find Me" Prov 8:17.

This passage of scripture also expresses a condition. It indicates to us that only certain ones, "those that seek Me early" will receive the desired result.

The Lord will share Himself with those who respond promptly to His "knocking." His approach to us may come in any one of many different forms or ways. Our ability to hear and rightly respond to His "knocking" can be cultivated. It is both possible and highly desirable that, as we satisfy the demands of our pattern of daily living, we learn to continually listen, should the Lord, desiring our fellowship, come and knock upon our heart's door.

> "The secret of the LORD is with them that fear Him *(a reverence that results in unquestioning trust and obedience)*; and He will shew them His covenant" Ps 25:14.

To these, He is able to say:

> "Come, My beloved, let us go forth into the field; let us lodge in the villages. Let us get up early to the vineyards; let us see if the vine flourish, whether the tender grape appear, and the pomegranates bud forth: there will I give thee My loves" SS 7:11-12.

Our Lord is seeking out those who will respond promptly to His knock on the door of their heart. He is searching for a Bride who is willing to respond to His presence **whenever He may choose** to come. As she invites Him to enter the room of her spiritual life, He will reciprocate by sharing with her His burden concerning His vineyard.

"Come, My beloved, let us go forth." She must "come" to Him first. Then together, they will be able to "go." This foundational principle, when understood, will strengthen our relationship with the Lord, and lead us toward spiritual maturity. As we respond to His call to "come" and then turn aside with Him for times of fellowship in His chambers, He will share His secrets and burdens with us. Only then will we be ready to cooperate with Him in ministry.

Throughout the Song of Songs, we find this principle in operation as the Bridegroom, due to His intense desire to be with her, came again and again seeking fellowship with His Bride. We are also able to see the problems that resulted from the reluctance of the Bride to respond to the Bridegroom's approaches when He returned and knocked upon the door of her heart at a very inconvenient time.

The development of her capacity to recognize His presence, and the "chastenings" that produced the motivation which would enable her to promptly respond to His presence at any time are clearly laid out for our meditation. We can learn much as we observe her mistakes and consider the means the Lord used to bring about the necessary correction within her. This will help us in our ability to rightly respond to His presence, as He seeks our fellowship.

After a time of fellowship with the Bride in the "Garden inclosed," the Bridegroom withdrew His presence and left her there, alone. During their time of intimate communion, the Lord received from her "something" that was very special and meaningful to Him. This is better understood by considering the following verse: "Behold, I stand at the door, and knock: if any man (or woman) hear My voice, and open the door, I will come in to him, and will sup with him, and he with Me" Rev 3:20. He had "supped" with His Bride and said concerning it, "I have gathered My myrrh with My spice; I have eaten My honeycomb with My honey; I have drunk My wine with My milk" SS 5:1b. He partook of the quality of her spiritual life.

After His departure, the Bride quietly pondered all that the Bridegroom had spoken, and that which had been accomplished within her during their time together; and she felt a deep sense of satisfaction, peace, and rest.

> "A garden inclosed is My sister, My spouse; a spring shut up, a fountain sealed. Thy plants are an orchard of pomegranates, with pleasant fruits; camphire, with spikenard, spikenard and saffron; calamus and cinnamon, with all trees of frankincense; myrrh and aloes, with all the chief spices: a fountain of gardens, a well of living waters, and streams from Lebanon" SS 4:12-15.

She still felt the effect of His presence, and recognized that her spirit had been quickened while she was with Him. She was becoming sensitive to the realm of the supernatural:

> "I sleep, but my heart waketh" SS 5:2a.

As she rested upon her bed, she continued to meditate upon this blessed time of communion with the Bridegroom within the Garden of her being. All at once, she faintly heard His voice again desiring her fellowship.

> "It is the voice of my Beloved that knocketh, saying, Open to Me, My sister, My love, My dove, My undefiled: for My head is filled with dew, and My locks with the drops of the night" SS 5:2b.

She heard Him knock, but responded with an excuse,

> "I have put off my coat; how shall I put it on? I have washed my feet; how shall I defile them?" SS 5:3.

She acknowledged His desire to be with her, but was not willing to be inconvenienced by responding to Him now. She was quite satisfied and comfortable as she rested upon her bed and thought about her past time of fellowship with Him. Content with the memory of their past visit, she desired nothing further from Him. She was willing to live with "what had been."

Notice that she heard His knock and that her spirit

was willing to respond: "My heart waketh." But, her flesh was weak, and she was not inclined to be disturbed: "I sleep." There was still much that had to be accomplished within her in order to bring about the changes which would enable her to become the Bride that He desired.

He must have a Bride who would obediently welcome Him, whenever He chose to come and accompany Him with anticipation, wherever He desired to go.

"Come, My beloved, let us go forth into the field" SS 7:11a.

"Who is this that cometh up from the wilderness, leaning upon her Beloved?" SS 8:5a.

Notice that it is the Lord Who is knocking, actively desiring fellowship with His Bride. This reveals the other side of our seeking Him, and depicts our Lord as a seeking God Who aggressively longs to be with us. He created man in His own image and likeness, with the ability to know His voice, and with the capacity for intelligent, satisfying, communion with Him.

David spoke of this seeking heart of the Lord in Psalm 42:7a,

"Deep calleth unto deep."

"Deep calleth" speaks of our Lord as a seeking God. There is a "deep" within the very being of God that desires to fellowship with man. Therefore, He created within man the same depth of spirit—a capacity for communion to which He could relate, that He might find the fellowship and satisfaction that He desired.

Throughout the Scriptures, the Lord is revealed as a seeking God.

127

> "For the eyes of the LORD run to and fro through-
> out the whole earth, to shew Himself strong in the
> behalf of them whose heart is perfect toward Him" 2
> Chron 16:9a.

> "For the eyes of the Lord are over the righteous, and
> His ears are open unto their prayers" 1 Pet 3:12a.

At times we may feel the Lord does not notice us, or
that He is not interested in us as an individual. However, He is far more interested in us and in revealing
Himself to us, than we are in having Him do so.

The Lord intensely desires to bring us into an abiding experience of communion with Him that we might
become "one" with Him in the outworking of His purposes for mankind. Beyond this, He longs to draw us
apart to Himself within His chambers, where He can
reveal to us the eternal things of the Spirit.

A teacher in the Bible School that I attended gave
this example of the seeking heart of the Lord, and how
He apprehends us. This school had a long, winding
lane that led out to the highway. There were tall ever-
green trees on both sides, which were so thick, it was
difficult for light to penetrate through them at night.
One evening, the teacher was walking with his young
daughter, holding her hand. It was so dark that they
were unable to see one another. As they walked, he
suddenly let loose of her hand and stepped back. He
could vaguely see an outline of her and had to concen-
trate on her form so as not to lose sight of her. When
she realized that he was gone, and she was in the
darkness alone, she cried out, "Daddy, where are you?"
He intentionally did not answer her. She panicked and
started to run. Then he carefully stepped in front of her
so she would run into him. As she ran into his waiting
arms, she exclaimed, "Oh daddy, I found you."

This is the way the Lord is. We often start to run
without direction or purpose and the Lord places Him-

self in the very center of our path so we will run right into Him. We are seeking and finding a God Who has first sought us and found us. If our heart-interest is toward Him, we can trust Him to do this.

The first confession of the Bride had been, "My Beloved is mine." At that time in her experience, she was diligently seeking after all of the "things" He was able to give her to make her comfortable.

> "Because of the savour of Thy good ointments Thy name is as ointment poured forth, **therefore** do the virgins love Thee" SS 1:3.

She was saying, "Because of all of the things that I am receiving from You, I love You." She was spiritually content, resting in all those things which were provided at her request, during times that were convenient for her.

> "As the apple tree among the trees of the wood, so is my Beloved among the sons. I sat down under His shadow with great delight, and His fruit was sweet to my taste" SS 2:3.

A time came however, when all these "things" were removed, and she was completely alone in what seemed to be a place of spiritual darkness. All she was able to say was,

> "By night on my bed I sought Him . . . but I found Him not" SS 3:1.

In the darkness of this experience, none of her gifts would operate, nor could she "feel" the presence of the Lord. She felt within herself that the Lord had left her. Finally, as she struggled with all these feelings, she turned and began the search for the Lord Himself.

> "I sought Him Whom my soul loveth" SS 3:1b.

After this confession of her true need, and her expressed desire to seek Him alone, the Lord appeared to her in a sovereign visitation. As He came up from the wilderness, He revealed Himself to her in a demonstration of all His manifest glory and majestic power.

Now, He is going to test the sincerity of the declaration she had made (*"By night on my bed I sought Him"*), to see if she really meant it. So, He came to her in the night season, after she had retired, and knocked on her heart's door to let her know He was there to seek her fellowship. Previously, in a very similar situation, she had loudly proclaimed that she was desperately seeking Him, but had been unable to find Him. Now, the Lord is present, seeking her.

He is knocking on the door of the heart of His Bride, saying,

> "Open to Me, My sister, My love, My dove, My undefiled: for My head is filled with dew, and My locks with the drops of the night" SS 5:2b.

This reveals to us another spiritual principle. The Lord will often deliberately come to us at a time when we may be the least willing to respond to Him, or at a time when we are very much occupied with other things. He does this when we least expect Him, in order to see if we really care for Him more than we care for other things—to expose what really matters to us.

Notice that His head was filled with "dew." The Lord had been seeking for fellowship elsewhere, but had not been able to find it. Therefore, He returned to her. We seldom realize the crucial importance of being able to discern His presence, and of having the determined will to respond to His invitation to fellowship. These "night seasons" are a special time during which the Lord often comes and knocks on the door of our heart, desiring our fellowship. This again reveals to us that He is a seeking God Who searches out those who are willing to pay whatever price is required in order to respond to Him.

This importune knocking of the Lord on the door of our heart to seek a response from us, will reveal what is really important to us. More often than not we make some excuse as to why we cannot respond, or we delay our coming apart to be with Him. We may say to the Lord, "Maybe in a half hour, as I am very busy now." This indicates that something else is more important to us than the Lord Himself. Whatever it may be, it can be considered as being an idol in our lives.

We criticize the children of Israel for their idols, and do not realize we also may have our own. An idol is anything that becomes a substitute, or takes the place of the Lord in our lives. When the Lord reveals Himself to us, He expects a response. If we respond, "Yes, Lord, but . . ." and put Him off for some reason, that object or reason becomes as an idol.

When the Lord knocked on the door of the heart of His Bride and said, "Open to Me," she offered a reasonable excuse. This is the point at which we struggle or often fail—prompt obedience in responding to Him. No matter how valid our reasons may be, if He is truly the Lord of our lives then His desire for our attention or fellowship should rise above the right to our own personal comfort and privacy. Too easily, we become busy or preoccupied with many things, and then use these as an excuse for our unresponsiveness to the Lord. All these things must submit to His claim on our time.

It is not only the carnal or sinful things that keep us from responding to the presence of the Lord; it is often things that are good, legitimate, and necessary. Everything else must become secondary to our times of communion and fellowship with Him if we value the experience of His manifest presence in our daily pattern of life. If we intend to climb the stairs into the realm of identification with Him in His eternal purpose, we must learn to promptly respond to His desire to come within the room of our spiritual being, regardless of our pre-occupation.

She said to the Lord, "I have put off my coat; how shall I put it on? I have washed my feet; how shall I defile them?" SS 5:3. Here is the Lord of Glory knocking at the door of the heart of His Bride, seeking her attention. He was asking her to turn aside from whatever she was doing at the present moment, and separate herself unto Him for a time. She did not respond in "prompt obedience" to His knocking because to do so would have been very inconvenient to her personal comfort; it would have required her to get out of her warm, cozy bed. Her excuse was so weak, and hardly comparable to the vast possibilities which would have been made available to her, had she obeyed.

In the time in which she lived, their homes had dirt floors and open sandals were worn. Therefore, before she could retire for the night, she had to wash her feet. She was saying, "If I get out of bed to open the door, I will have to walk through the dirt and it will be necessary for me to wash my feet all over again. I just do not feel like doing this and besides, I am very tired." She was not willing to inconvenience her flesh.

Obedience to the Lord involves taking up a cross. Our natural being will always react to this. The Scripture says,

> "For the flesh lusteth against the Spirit, and the Spirit against the flesh: and these are **contrary** the one to the other: so that ye cannot do the things that ye would" Gal 5:17.

The inconveniences that we must overcome or endure in becoming obedient to the Lord is a very small price to pay in order to climb the stairs and enter into a very rewarding time of communion with Him in His chambers.

We must take up our cross and allow the fleshly desires and personal comforts of our souls to die upon it, whatever the cost may be. By a determined act of will, we must develop and maintain within us a "quality of spirit" that is both perceptive and receptive to hearing His voice, and which is continually poised toward Him. Then, when He knocks upon the door of our heart, we will be able to respond to Him and invite Him to come within the room of our spiritual life.

The excuse the Bride gave was both legitimate and true. Nevertheless, the Bridegroom was grieved due to the delay in her response, and He left. A way of entrance that leads to the secret place of the stairs had been placed in her path, but she failed to enter. The Lord even knocked on the door of her heart to help guide her to the secret place of entrance to these stairs that led upward into His chambers and purposes. He made it as easy as He could for her to ascend into the place He had prepared for her.

However, moving upward on these stairs affected her temporary personal comfort, so she did not obey and thus lost an eternal reward. By considering the consequences of her failure, we will be able to understand that our obedience to His promptings is far more important than we may have realized.

> "If ye be willing and obedient, ye shall eat the good of the land" Is 1:19.

The eternal gains that result from our willing obedience are far greater in value than any temporal comfort we may lose in seeking eternal things.

To answer His knock upon the door of our heart may open for us a realm of experience with Him that we have little expected, or even dreamed of.

Chapter 11

Distinctions That Make A Difference

"There are threescore queens . . .
My dove, My undefiled is but one"
SS 6:8a, 9a.

The certainty that all Christians experience the "abiding presence" of the Holy Spirit is absolute. There are no conditions to meet, apart from receiving Jesus as Savior. For all who are redeemed, the indwelling presence of the Holy Spirit is a reality that can be depended upon. The Holy Spirit is always faithful in His ministry of maintaining our redemption and of making Jesus known to us, and very real within us.

However, the possibility of our experiencing the "manifest presence" of Jesus is conditional. To have the ability to recognize His personal presence when He comes and knocks on the door of our heart, and the capability of being able to rightly respond to Him when He does, is dependent upon the "set of our spirit" and upon the development of our spiritual sensitivity.

This means that we must prayerfully keep our spirit poised upward, so we will be able to "sense" His presence when He comes to make known His desire to fellowship with us.

As our love for Jesus grows, we should find ourselves expectantly looking forward to these visitations of His manifest presence. This requires our learning how to open the "door of entrance" into our inner spiritual being to the Lord, when He comes.

In our new birth, we become a spiritual being—a new creation (2 Cor 5:17-18a). Our spirit has newly born senses that must be developed, just as our natural senses gradually matured as we grew.

> "There is a natural body, and there is a spiritual body" 1 Cor 15:44b.

It is through these inner spiritual senses that we perceive, or recognize the manifest presence of the Lord.

> "Behold, I stand at the door, and knock" Rev 3:20a.

Those who truly desire His friendship will quickly respond to the manifestation of the fact of His presence *(knocking)*, and invite Him to come within the "room" of their spiritual being. This room *(chamber)* is the area within our inner being where we commune with the Lord. It is a "set apart" place where He is alone with us *(our chamber)*, and where we are alone with Him *("His chambers")*. As we expectantly invite the Lord to come within "our chamber" to sup with us, He will guide us to the stairs that lead upward to "His chambers" where we sup with Him, and from which we go with Him into the vineyards.

The Heavenly Bridegroom attempted to visit His Bride at a time that happened to be inconvenient for her, therefore she failed to respond. Disappointed, He departed because of her reluctance to open "the door of her chamber" to fellowship with Him. But, all was not lost. Instead, He allowed her to recognize the essential difference that exists between the gifts and blessings that He willingly left behind for her to find, and the tremendous value of His "manifest presence." Jesus longs for us to desire to know Him as a Person, rather than only for what He can provide.

During the time in which the Bride lived, the latch on the door of entrance into her home was located on the inside of the door. It could only be unlatched by reaching through a small hole in the door and unlocking it from within. This provided a limited means of security and protection.

The Lord so intensely desired to be with His Bride that He reached through this opening in the door toward the latch, but would not open it. The "door of entrance" to our spiritual chamber is always within our control, and may only be opened by us. This action by the Lord of reaching toward the Bride deeply stirred her. Later, she testified concerning this,

> "My Beloved put in His hand by the hole of the door, and my bowels *(the inner depths of her being)* were moved for Him" SS 5:4.

The Lord will never invade or violate our privacy. We must open the door; He never will. This principle is established in Scripture.

> "**If** any man **hear** My voice, and **open** the door, I will come in to him" Rev 3:20b.

When she noticed that His hand was reaching toward the latch as an expression of His desire toward her, she *(finally)* responded and opened the door to Him.

> "I rose up to open to my Beloved; and my hands dropped with myrrh, and my fingers with sweet smelling myrrh, upon the handles of the lock. I

opened to my Beloved; but my Beloved had withdrawn Himself, and was gone: my soul failed when
He spake: I sought Him, but I could not find Him; I
called Him, but He gave me no answer" SS 5:5-6.

When she opened the door, He was no longer there.
Because of the delay in her response, He had reluctantly withdrawn His "manifest presence" from the
door of entrance into her chamber. Yet the anointing, or
the result of His presence, had remained upon the lock.
When she touched the lock, all of this anointing came
onto her hands. She had a "handful" of the blessings
that He left behind when He departed. Previously, she
would have been content to have these apart from Him.
Now, she panicked and longed for the personal presence of the Bridegroom Himself.

Many are not able to differentiate between these two
aspects of His presence. First, there is the general
sense of His Divine presence that relates to our salvation, and to its outworking within our lives. This
speaks of the unconditional, "abiding presence" of the
Holy Spirit within us.

Second, there is the coming of the Lord to us as a
Person having intellect, will, and emotions. The Lord is
eager to come within our chamber, and personally
share Himself with us in fellowship. Along with this,
He will lead us upward into His chambers and allow
us to share with Him in the outworking of His eternal
purposes. This speaks of a "conditional" visitation from
the Lord to us, and is referred to as His "manifest
presence."

The first aspect of His presence is general, and relates to His redemptive grace.

"Do not I fill heaven and earth? saith the LORD" Jer
23:24b.

The second aspect of His presence is specific, and relates to His Person.

> "He standeth behind our wall, He looketh forth at the windows, shewing Himself through the lattice" SS 2:9b *(see also John 14:21-23).*

The experience of her failure in responding to the attempted visit of the Bridegroom became a very important step for the Bride in learning the secret *(a prompt response to His manifest presence)* that leads to ascent up the stairs into His chambers. She had missed her opportunity to respond to the manifest presence of the Lord this time, but she learned through her disobedience that she urgently needed to develop an inner spiritual sensitivity so she would be able to hear His knocking upon the door of her chamber. She also learned the importance of quickly responding to His approaches, regardless of her present circumstances.

> "I love them that love Me; and those that **seek Me early** *(without delay)* shall find Me" Prov 8:17.

Previously, the Bride had picturesquely described a characteristic of the Bridegroom—His hesitation in revealing Himself because of His sensitivity to being rejected. She had said,

> "My Beloved is like a roe or a young hart" SS 2:9a.

She recognized that His manifest presence was delicate, and could be easily grieved. Thus, she should have known that He would leave when she delayed in responding to Him.

We should learn from her mistake so we do not become the cause of another disappointment to the Lord. We must be diligent to become more perceptive so we will be able to discern His presence. We need to be attentive in our "listening" for His knock, so we will be able to promptly turn aside from whatever we are doing, when He comes to reveal Himself to us. Then, in anticipation, we can invite Him to come within the "chamber" of our spiritual being.

After her failure to respond promptly to His visitation, the Bride made a second mistake. Instead of asking for His forgiveness, requesting another visitation, and waiting for Him to come again, she returned to her old ways and went to others for advice concerning the loss of His presence.

> "The watchmen that went about the city found me, they smote me, they wounded me; the keepers of the walls took away my veil from me" SS 5:7.

Again, the ministry turned on her because of her disobedience. They did not understand the "inner workings" that were moving within her being at this particular time to bring about the changes that would enable her to become responsive to the Lord.

> "For we are His workmanship, created in Christ Jesus unto good works, which God hath before ordained that we should walk in them" Eph 2:10.

Unseen to these watchmen, the Lord was diligently at work deep within her being. He was enlarging within her the desire to maintain an attitude of expectancy concerning His visits to her. Along with this, He was creating within her the ability to better respond to and move with, His manifest presence. These watchmen only looked on the surface problem, which was not the true, inner need that was disturbing her. Therefore, they made her condition worse. There are times when the Lord alone can help us through difficult circumstances.

The Lord left her in this condition for a while. This time, her visit to these watchmen had a different outcome. Her heart had been captivated by the Lord and she was earnestly searching for Him, rather than frantically seeking for His blessings as in the past. Therefore, she recognized that the Lord was allowing her to be chastened through the ministry, that she might be inwardly changed.

She had come to understand that the Lord works "all things together for good." Therefore, she was able to maintain a good attitude toward these watchmen. We also must be very careful about giving expression to our feelings concerning difficult situations in which we find ourselves, especially when others seemingly do not understand. It is exceedingly important that we discipline ourselves in order to maintain the sensitivity of our spirit to His presence.

After this experience with the watchmen, she turned to those who should have been seeking Him with her, and said to them,

> "I charge you, O Daughters of Jerusalem, if ye find my Beloved, that ye tell Him, that I am sick of love" SS 5:8.

There are two different categories of Christians within the Church. This is clearly demonstrated in the Song of Solomon.

> "My dove, My undefiled is but one; she is the only one of her mother, she is the choice one of her that bare her. The Daughters saw her, and blessed her" SS 6:9a.

The first is the "Bride"—the Church within the Church. This hidden "Church within" is first known to the Lord. The "visible Church," the Daughters of Jerusalem, are first seen by man.

The Bride has captured the singular attention and

141

interest of the Bridegroom. She said to the Lord,

> "Tell me, O Thou Whom my soul loveth, where Thou feedest, where Thou makest Thy flock to rest at noon: for why should I be as one that turneth aside by the flocks of Thy companions?" SS 1:7.

She is not satisfied with simply enjoying the blessings of salvation and with having a part in the program of the Church. She reaches beyond others to the Lord Himself.

The second group, the "Daughters of Jerusalem," are saved and have some understanding of the things of God. They attend church and become involved, to a certain extent, but are satisfied with being saved, healed, and blessed. These say to the Bride,

> "What is thy Beloved more than another beloved" SS 5:9a.

They are saying, "We have gone far enough, we will stay here. Besides, we do not see why we need to go through all those dealings, like you do."

The Bride was seeking the Lord because He had withdrawn His "manifest presence" from her. She could no longer be satisfied with the church program, as the Daughters of Jerusalem were. Therefore, she was searching for the Lord of the program and spoke to the "Church visible"—portrayed here as the "Daughters of Jerusalem"—and said to them,

> "I charge you, O Daughters of Jerusalem, if ye find my Beloved, that ye tell Him, that I am sick of love" SS 5:8.

The Daughters of Jerusalem *(Church visible)* answered her and said,

> "What is thy Beloved more than another beloved, O

thou fairest among women? What is thy Beloved
more than another beloved, that thou dost so charge
us?" SS 5:9.

They only saw the benefits of being a Christian. To
them, going to church represented an obligation or
duty. Also, it provided them with a time for social
fellowship and activities. The thought of fellowship and
communion with the Lord Himself was far from their
minds, or interest. They could only say to the Bride,
"What is He more than a good job, a nice home, or
security? What is He more than all of the good things
we have? We are satisfied and content. We are the
'Daughters of Jerusalem' *(saved)*, and it is enough. Do
not bother us with your seeking of the Lord, you are
trying to be too spiritual."

But something had happened within the being of the
Bride. She had been in the garden alone with Him, and
had experienced the joy and the satisfaction of communion with Him. Now, she longed for the continuing
experience of His personal presence and friendship.
She felt incomplete when she was apart from Him.
When the Daughters of Jerusalem said to her, "What is
He more than another," she did not tell them about all
the blessings she had received from Him. Rather, she
began to extol the Bridegroom Himself.

"My Beloved is white and ruddy, the chiefest among
ten thousand. His head is as the most fine gold, His
locks are bushy, and black as a raven. His eyes are
as the eyes of doves by the rivers of waters, washed
with milk, and fitly set. His cheeks are as a bed of
spices, as sweet flowers: His lips like lilies, dropping
sweet smelling myrrh. His hands are as gold rings
set with the beryl: His belly is as bright ivory overlaid
with sapphires. His legs are as pillars of marble, set
upon sockets of fine gold: His countenance is as
Lebanon, excellent as the cedars. His mouth is most
sweet: yea, He is altogether lovely. This is my Beloved,

and this is my Friend, O Daughters of Jerusalem"
SS 5:10-16.

She had been spending time alone with her beloved,
the Lord Jesus Christ, and was able to give an intimate
description of Him. She could clearly describe His Person because she had a single eye toward Him. She
knew Him as an intimate friend, and could give a clear,
authoritative expression to His beauty and to His desirability.

The Daughters of Jerusalem had said,

"What is thy Beloved more than another beloved,
that thou dost so charge us?" SS 5:9b.

The Bride with heart-authority, due to her personal
knowledge and relationship with Him, exalted the Lord
Jesus and set Him forth as the answer to the inner cry
of every heart. This brought a response from the
Daughters of Jerusalem which is so needed in our day
of special gimmicks and programs that are being used
to build up the Church.

"Whither is thy Beloved gone, O thou fairest among
women? whither is thy Beloved turned aside? that
we may seek Him with thee?" SS 6:1.

Their spirit had been stirred by the testimony that
flowed out of the Bride as she gave expression to her
love for Him. She set forth the Lord Himself in evident
view for the Daughters of Jerusalem to behold. In Acts
1:8a the Lord said, "But ye shall receive power, after
that the Holy Ghost is come upon you: and ye shall be
witnesses **unto Me**." Only as we become so close to
Him that we can express our witness "unto Him" will
His beauty be reflected through us for others to behold.

The enemy of our spiritual life seeks to turn us aside
from this, and will try to tell us: "It is selfish to en-

144

deavor to **become** spiritual, or to spend time 'waiting on the Lord.' Rather, go out and **do** something for somebody else. Get so busy working for the Lord that you have no time to prepare yourself to work with Him." The enemy knows the power that can flow through the life of one who has been alone with the Lord in His chambers. He knows the heart cry of those who will eagerly respond—when they witness the beauty of Jesus being expressed through the life of His Bride.

> "Whither is thy Beloved gone, O thou fairest among women? whither is thy Beloved turned aside? **that we may seek Him with thee**" SS 6:1.

We must purposely set apart time to wait upon the Lord. As we do, we will fall so completely in love with Jesus and we will become so like Him, that it will be He that is seen, rather than us. Then, wherever we go, His presence that abides with us will cut through every hindering bondage and every fear in those who are witnessing the result of His life in ours. This will bring others to a knowledge of Jesus Christ.

> "For many are called, but few are chosen" Matt 22:14.

The "many" refers to the Daughters of Jerusalem. The "few" refers to the Bride. Another way to say this is: "The Daughters of Jerusalem are called, but a Bride is being chosen out from among them, because she has become willing to come apart and seek Him."

> "There are threescore queens . . . My dove, My undefiled is but one" SS 6:8a, 9a.

Here again, two different categories are expressed. The called, and the chosen. The "called" includes all Christians. The "chosen" refers to those who have pressed on to know the Lord Himself. These have discovered "the secret of the stairs," and have begun their upward climb into His chambers to be with Him.

The Lord is calling a Bride out from among those who are still saying, "I have gone to bed, how shall I get up?" These "Daughters of Jerusalem" know the voice of the Lord to a degree, but they are not committed. They have a limited involvement in the Church and are willing to go only so far. Here, they draw a line and refuse to go further. They say, "I will not become one of those fanatics." They know there is a price to pay in order to enter His chambers, and they are not willing to pay it.

"The Daughters saw her, and blessed her" SS 6:9b.

These have enough spiritual capacity to recognize the Bride, and enough spiritual sense to know they should bless her. However, they can only see the Lord through the description that the Bride willingly shares with them when she, with a glow within her being, says to them, "This is my Beloved, and this is my Friend, O Daughters of Jerusalem."

How much better it is to arise from our bed of indifference to respond to His knocking on the door of our heart, and then allow Him to guide us upward on the stairs into His chambers that we might come to intimately know Him; and, in the manifestation of His presence, to share together with Him in His purposes.

He longs to be able to say to us:

"Come, My beloved, let us go forth into the field; let us lodge in the villages. Let us get up early to the vineyards; let us see if the vine flourish, whether the tender grape appear, and the pomegranates bud forth: **there will I give thee My loves**" SS 7:11-12.

Chapter 12

Satisfaction
And Responsibility
In Attainment

"I am my Beloved's, and His desire is toward me"
SS 7:10.

This is the third and final confession of the Bride. It reveals to us the extent of the complete change that has taken place within her. She has come to the place in her experience where she no longer needs to make demands on the Lord in order to find satisfaction. Rather, she has totally made herself available to Him for His purposes. Her self-life has been dealt with, and is no longer a hindrance to their times of communion.

Finally, the Lord may expect a prompt and favorable response from His Bride at any time that He knocks on the door of her heart. With confidence He now invites her to come apart from her activities in order to be with Him, knowing this is her desire also. In anticipation He can say to her,

"Come, My beloved, let **us** go forth into the field; let **us** lodge in the villages. Let us get up early to the vineyards; let **us** see if the vine flourish, whether the tender grape appear, and the pomegranates bud forth: **there** will I give thee My loves" SS 7:11-12.

As they walked through the vineyards together, the Bride became aware of a need which she shared with the Lord.

> **"We** have a little sister, and she hath no breasts: what shall **we** do for **our** sister in the day when she shall be spoken for?" SS 8:8.

She may now approach the Lord at any time, to request His wisdom in behalf of the one for whom she is burdened; and with confidence she expects a prompt response from Him, knowing this is His desire also. In anticipation, she can quietly wait until He responds in love, and with concern for the burden she feels.

The Lord quickly responded to her question, "What shall we do?" He replied,

> "If she be a wall, **we** will build upon her a palace of silver: and if she be a door, **we** will inclose her with boards of cedar" SS 8:9.

His answer was practical and dealt with the root of the problem—her spiritual immaturity, rather than the obvious, "She hath no breasts." Then He offered to work with His Bride to bring about the necessary correction.

The Lord's answer set forth the spiritual principles that applied to this situation. Along with this, He revealed the course of action that should be taken concerning the need of this "little sister."

First, He exposed her deficiency in foundational truth; she was unstable, like a "swinging door." This resulted in her lack of spiritual growth (*she did not have* breasts). Then, the Lord voiced a "word of knowledge," revealing the way to effectively bring about the needed correction: "We will inclose her with boards of cedar."

148

The solution involved correcting this little sister's instability through teaching and quiet meditation. She would become immovable, as a wall, protected from temptation *(enclosed in boards of cedar)* while this foundation for her faith was being established within her. After this was accomplished, a further work was needed. A habitation *(chamber)* for the Lord was to be built upon it, "We will build upon her a palace of silver."

Our salvation experience is merely the beginning of the complete work which the Lord desires to do within each of us.

> "Now therefore ye are no more strangers and for-eigners, but fellowcitizens with the saints, and of the household of God; and are built upon the foundation of the apostles and prophets, Jesus Christ Himself being the chief corner stone; in Whom all the building fitly framed together **groweth** unto an holy temple in the Lord: in Whom ye also are builded together for an habitation of God through the Spirit" Eph 2:19-22.

The Lord and His Bride will cooperate *("We will")* in the outworking of the answer. The vision of the Bride-groom, along with the burden of the Bride, are merged into a single concern for this little one who is immature. While He ministers His love to the Bride *("There will I give thee My loves")*, together they will minister their love to this little sister until she matures.

No longer need the Bride say,

> "My mother's children were angry with me; **they** made me the keeper of the vineyards" SS 1:6b.

She has learned the secret of entrance into His chambers and has experienced the joy of working "with" Him, rather than "for" Him. The "anger" and the "pressure" of duty is gone, and in its place is the inner peace and fulfillment that result from their working together.

"There will I give thee My loves" SS 7:12b.

The Lord revealed the spiritual principles that relate to this need; **"If** she be a wall, we will build," or, **"If** she be a door, we will inclose." Then He waited for the Bride to determine which of these, a door or a wall, expressed the present condition and need of this young Christian. The Lord was beginning to introduce His Bride to a place of spiritual responsibility in His Kingdom.

The first possibility *("If she be a wall")* speaks of stability in our salvation experience as a result of our understanding and having faith in the foundational doctrines upon which we stand. As these basic principles are established in our life experience, then the Lord will be able to build upon this foundation (see Matt 7:24-29).

The Lord speaks of that which is to be built upon this foundation as a "palace of silver." This visible "witness" comes into being through the building up of the quality and the character of our spiritual life. The spiritual maturity which is being developed within our lives should appear to others as a "palace of silver." This involves righteous deeds, or right living, in our daily pattern of life. The foundation upon which this spiritual growth is to be built is extremely important. Otherwise, the manifestation of our spiritual life would be faulty, and we might be viewed by others as a "shanty of lead" rather than as a "palace of silver."

The second possibility, "If she be a door," refers to spiritual instability. This confused state of being comes about through a faulty understanding of foundational doctrines, or an uncertainty concerning spiritual experiences. Such confusion would cause her to function like a door that is hung with double-swing hinges so it can open, first one way, and then suddenly the opposite way. This "swinging door" condition would require a constant vigilance and care over her until a degree of stability could be developed in her spiritual experience. Therefore, the Lord said that she was to be "enclosed in boards of cedar."

Being enclosed with boards of cedar speaks of pastoral protection until this "little sister" that is within each one of us has been able to dig down through the "rubble" that hinders our spiritual growth. This rubble may have accumulated within us due to a failure in the outworking of our faith, or from prayers that were not answered as we expected. It could have resulted from a spiritual experience that did not produce the expected results and left us confused. It might be caused by defects in our understanding of spiritual principles, which would lead us to feel the Lord does not care about us.

These conditions can result in distrust and doubts about the supernatural, and produce a spiritual cloudiness within us. The protection, guidance, and love that is extended to this little sister will both encourage her, and give her time to dig down through all this mixture in her spiritual experience to the solid Rock that is beneath. Then, she will be able to stand firmly on this Rock Foundation, our Lord Jesus Christ. No longer will she be seen as a swinging door.

The needs of this "little sister" were met because of the close relationship between the Bridegroom and the Bride. The Bride has come into an experience of direct communion with the Bridegroom, and is willing to respond to His every desire, as when He said to her,

"Come, My beloved, let us go forth into the field" SS 7:11a.

The Bridegroom is in direct communion with the Bride and is waiting to respond to her every desire, as when she said to Him, "We have a little sister, what shall we do for her?" This cooperative relationship between the Bridegroom and the Bride has gradually developed into a beautifully productive communion. Such needs as this can now be met as together each contributes their part.

This came about as the result of an ongoing process in which the Bride was being gradually drawn by the Bridegroom, step upon step, into His chambers. He had continued to approach the Bride again and again, knocking upon the door of her heart, seeking entrance into her life. The Bride, through lessons consisting of many failures and mistakes had learned to recognize His presence and to respond promptly. In time, her obedience resulted in an "open door" to her heart, through which the Lord could enter at will and invite His Bride to "rise up and come away" with Him for whatever purpose He had in view at that time.

This open door into the heart and life of His Bride, which was gained by the Lord's unceasing perseverance, has also benefited her. Now she may approach Him whenever she wishes to ask His counsel and help concerning the needs for which she has a burden. The complete change in her is apparent, for we recall that in the beginning she sought to possess the Bridegroom and said, "He is mine." At that time, she was content with the things He provided, and willingly abode alone in His shadow.

This did not discourage the Lord, however, for He patiently led His Bride step upon step, upward into His chambers, where she could "sup" with Him.

"I love them that love Me; and those that seek Me early shall find Me . . . that I may cause those that love Me to inherit **substance**; and I will fill their treasures" Prov 8:17, 21a.

As a result of the "substance" received during these times of "supping" with the Bridegroom, she had grown into a fully developed, cooperative relationship that held special meaning and purpose both to herself, and to the Lord.

Of this fully-developed relationship with the Lord, the Bride testifies:

"I am a wall, and my breasts like towers" SS 8:10.

Now, all the "little sisters" will be able to receive from her the "substance" they desperately need so they may grow into the same stature of spiritual maturity as she. Not only does she have this ability to feed others; she is able to fulfill a desire that was within the Lord when He came to walk with Adam in the Garden of Eden.

When tested, Adam failed; but the Bride, through testing, has proved herself to be qualified. Therefore, her spiritual walk is now as stable as a "wall." The Lord, with confidence may say to His Bride,

"How beautiful are thy feet with shoes, O prince's daughter!" SS 7:1a.

He can come in "the cool of the day" Gen 3:8, and she will be there, ready to walk with Him through the vineyards, seeking others who desire to be nurtured and brought to the level of spiritual maturity she now enjoys.

Before we may enter into the full experience of becoming espoused to our Heavenly Bridegroom, it is necessary that we qualify. The outworking of this qualifying process is revealed to us through the progression in the Bride's experience, as expressed in the Song of

Solomon. This processing began when she, one of the many Daughters of Jerusalem, began to see the Bridegroom with a "single eye" and said to Him, "Draw me, we *(all of me)* will run after Thee." This touched His heart, and He began to see her with a "single eye." She had gained His approbation, or favor.

Now the Lord was moved to become active within her life's circumstances to bring about the progressive changes that were confirmed by each of her three testimonies. Her response to His presence, along with her obedience to the "dealings" that caused, or enabled these necessary changes to take place, qualified her to enter each higher level of experience with the Lord, as she ascended the stairs. This is the reason for the "secret" concerning the stairs. The way of entrance and ascent to His chambers is revealed only to those who seek Him with this "single eye" by sincerely praying, "Draw me." This must be followed by a heart commitment to a "willing obedience" that enables us to "run after Him."

To better understand this "conditional" relationship, it is helpful to consider the spiritual condition of those who have **not** qualified to be His Bride. The distinction between the two is particularly evident as we compare the spiritual position, experience, and perspective of the Bride to that of the Daughters of Jerusalem.

The Bride had **direct** access to the Lord through her personal relationship with Him. She was able to give a very intimate description of Him, and of the resultant blessings of her communion with Him. She expressed to the Daughters of Jerusalem a very detailed description of His Person and His desirability. She could say from experience,

> "His mouth is most sweet: yea, He is altogether lovely. This is my Beloved, and this is my Friend, O

Daughters of Jerusalem" SS 5:16.

The Daughters of Jerusalem had **indirect** access to the Lord through their relationship to the Bride. The only vision they had of the Lord was that which they received through the Bride. The Daughters had access to the Lord only through the Bride.

> "Whither is thy Beloved gone, O thou fairest among women? whither is thy Beloved turned aside? that we may seek Him with thee" SS 6:1.

The only direct description the Daughters were able to give was the Bride's, from whom they drew their spiritual life.

> "The Daughters saw her, and blessed her; yea, the queens and the concubines, and they praised her" SS 6:9b.

This difference in how the Bride and the Daughters saw the Lord resulted in a very noticeable difference in their relationship to Him. The Bride was enjoying the personal presence of the Lord, and was involved with Him in a ministry in the Vineyards. She could speak directly to Him and express the burden of her heart, "We have a little sister, what can we do for her?" The Daughters of Jerusalem were mainly concerned with things of lesser importance and could only say to the Bride,

> "What is thy Beloved more than another beloved, O thou fairest among women? what is thy Beloved more than another beloved, that thou dost so charge us?" SS 5:9.

Within each Christian body are two representative groups that are similar, yet different from each other. There is a group much like these Daughters of Jerusalem. They see the Lord, but only through the lives of others *(His Bride)*, who live so close to Him that, as a mirror, they reflect His Person and presence. Even as the "Daughters of Jerusalem" were busy with other things, these are content with the memory of their past experiences. They receive their spiritual nourishment from the Bride; and, because they greatly affect her spiritual life and walk, the Bride has much to overcome.

These Daughters of Jerusalem had said to the Bride, "What is He more than another?" Their testimony expressed the reality of their salvation, but it was evident that they had not grown beyond this point. They chose to live in comfort, as it pleased them, and had not submitted their lives to the processings of the Lord that lead to His chambers. They did not make themselves available to be disciplined by the Lord as the Bride had. Rather, having spent their lifetime accumulating the riches of this world, they had failed to purchase eternal things.

There is today an innumerable company of believers who, like these Daughters, sense that there is something more to life than all that they possess. These are searching for Him, and are catching His eye and interest.

> "Whither is thy Beloved turned aside? that we may seek Him with thee" SS 6:1b.

These are being called **out from among** the Daughters by the Lord to go through a time of preparation, in order to become a part of His Bride. These He will soon call to "rise up and come away." It is obvious that the Daughters of Jerusalem will be left behind when this takes place.

We are making our decisions concerning eternity now. The time that we have been given here on earth in order to make these choices is the most important time of all eternity.

"In my Father's house are many mansions" John 14:2a.

This verse can be expressed in another way: "There are many different levels of spiritual attainment to which we can ascend, by entering 'the secret of the stairs.'" The vertical level that we attain, as a result of the total of our lifetime decisions and experiences, will become the horizontal level upon which we will move throughout eternity. The "height" to which we have attained will be determined by the cumulative result of our choices, decisions, and attitudes toward the things of God here in this life.

This is the importance of understanding the "secret" of the stairs. Each step on the stairs brings us upward into a new level. As we ascend to each new level, our revelation and experience must be tested and proven. In heaven, there is no suffering, no temptation, and no devil to try us. It is here in this life, as we continue our ascent up the stairs, and are faithful in our times of testing, that our being "called" by the Lord will be changed into being "chosen" by Him to become His Bride.

"For many are called, but few are chosen" Matt 22:14.

We are to continue climbing these stairs. If we say, "This is as far as I am going," then throughout all eternity we will move on that parallel level, while another may have gone higher. In Eternity, it is too late to go higher. Paul said,

"If by any means I might attain unto the resurrection of the dead" Phil 3:11.

He was speaking of an out-resurrection from among the living dead, a resurrection from among the Daughters of Jerusalem up into the Bride. Paul saw the difference in these groups and he sought the higher level. Therefore he said,

> "I press toward the mark for the prize of the high calling of God in Christ Jesus" Phil 3:14.

The first confession of the Bride had been, "My Beloved is mine" SS 2:16a. She possessed Him and was busy at work for Him, but had no relationship with Him. Nevertheless, through progressive dealings, she came to the place where she found she could only be satisfied with Him. Then her confession became, "I am my Beloved's, and my Beloved is mine" SS 6:3a. Once she had personally met Him, she placed Him first in her life.

The Lord began to escort her to yet another step. She was again led into the wilderness that she might experience a total dependence upon Him. The Daughters saw this and said,

> "Who is this that cometh up from the wilderness, leaning upon her Beloved?" SS 8:5a.

Now, the Bride was able to say, "I am my Beloved's, and His desire is toward me." He had become her all in all and could say to her, "Come, My beloved, let us go forth into the field."

The call of God is never to "go," it is always to "come." When the Lord called Moses to deliver His people from Egypt, He said to Moses, "**Come** now therefore, and I will send thee unto Pharaoh" Ex 3:10a. The call to "come" involved his preparation for the sending forth. When Peter was called, Jesus said, "Come ye after Me, and I will **make you to become** fishers of men" Mark 1:17b. If we are faithful in our "coming," the Lord will be faithful in sending us. All too few are "sent" in our day because they failed to first "come."

The Lord said, "Come, My beloved, let us go forth into the field . . . there will I give thee My loves." This "field" speaks of our place of service. Her mother's children had forced her to keep the vineyard. Now the Lord is leading her into the vineyard, "Come . . . let us go forth." No longer is she working **for** the Lord; she is working in Divine union **with** Him.

Because of this progression in purpose and goal, the Bride faces a greater measure of responsibility. The Scripture tells us,

> "For unto whomsoever much is given, of him shall be much required" Luke 12:48b.

With privilege comes responsibility. The Lord places much responsibility on those whom He knows and can trust.

> "Solomon had a vineyard at Baal-hamon; he let out the vineyard unto keepers; every one for the fruit thereof was to bring a thousand pieces of silver" SS 8:11.

The Lord expects those who know Him and have understanding in His ways to bring forth a very fruitful harvest. From the fruit of their harvest, He expects to receive "a thousand pieces of silver" as His portion.

The Bride also had a vineyard—the Daughters of Jerusalem—for whom she was responsible.

> "My vineyard, which is mine, is before me: Thou, O Solomon, must have a thousand, and those that keep the fruit thereof two hundred" SS 8:12.

She was expected to provide Solomon with "a thousand" from her vineyard, while those who were dependent upon her were only required to supply "two hundred." More was required of her because He personally worked with her in the vineyard.

As we spend time with the Lord in His chambers, our capacity is enlarged and we become capable of accomplishing much more in His vineyard. We have direct access to His wisdom and therefore are able to produce much more. Although greater responsibility is involved, the joy of communion with Him makes it all worthwhile.

If we are true to all we have been taught, the day will come when we will hear with gladness,

> "Well done, good and faithful servant; thou hast been faithful over a few things, I will make thee ruler over many things: enter thou into the joy of thy Lord" Matt 25:23.

Let us respond to His knocking upon the door of our heart, and begin the upward ascent on the stairs, one step at a time, until we stand before Him in our Bridal garments, awaiting our marriage to Him.

That will be a glorious day.

Conclusion

The purpose of the Lord in preserving the manuscript of the Song of Solomon to become a part of our Bible extends far beyond the knowledge which can be gleaned from it concerning Solomon seeking after the Shulamite. The message that lives within the pages of this book transcends time and reaches out to touch our lives, just as though we were this Shulamite.

As we have prayerfully meditated upon the Song of Solomon, we discovered that this "Bride to be" was patiently being drawn by the Lord through a series of progressive processings.

First, she was separated from among the Daughters of Jerusalem. Then, she was delivered from all of her self-centered seeking. Finally, with a single eye, she began to long for the personal presence of the Bridegroom.

In the same way, we also will be "processed" by the Lord, if we intend to become a part of His Bride. Each one who has this desire will progress through, in some measure, this experience of a double separation.

These will be drawn out from among the present-day "Daughters of Jerusalem" and set free from all that is less than His best. Then, as in that day, they will be seen coming up out of the wilderness of our day, "leaning" upon their Beloved.

These "dealings" will require much from each one

who desires to become a part of this corporate Bride that is yet being prepared, of whom the Scripture says:

> "Blessed are they which are called unto the marriage supper of the Lamb" Rev 19:9b.

The love-relationship that developed between the Bridegroom and this one who captivated His heart is laid out before us in explicit poetic form within the pages of this book. The capacity to experience this same beautiful love-relationship with the Lord is being developed within those who are presently asking to be drawn to Him, and are determined to run after Him.

These are finding their way upward on the stairs and into His chambers, where they will experience an inner satisfaction and fulfillment that far transcends all that this world may offer.

All of this preparation begins with the piece of "raw material" that we are: our experience of salvation, the spiritual gifts that we have, all of our self-centeredness and problems. Then progressively, we will be enabled to discover the "secrets" that will set us free from these, and carry us upward toward union with Him in His chambers.

To those who have been touched by the searching love of this Heavenly Bridegroom, and who have a compelling desire to intimately know Him, the pages of this book will become brightly illuminated. They will unfold, revealing the secret key that unlocks the door of entrance into the progressive "workings" that will prepare each of those who have touched His heart, that they might be presented to Him as a Bride—made ready for that day.

If this is your heart's desire, and if you have not yet found the way upward on the stairs that lead to His chambers, then prayerfully re-read the pages of this book, personally, intimately, placing yourself in the "shoes" of the "Bride-to-be" who lives within the Song of Solomon, and walk with her, step by step, through all that brought her to Him.

To all others, the pages of this book will be but a record of Solomon seeking after the Shulamite.

> "And the *(His)* disciples came, and said unto Him, Why speakest Thou unto them in parables? He answered and said unto them, Because it is given unto **you to know the mysteries** of the Kingdom of Heaven, but to **them** it is not given" Matt 13:10-11.

Blessed are the **"YOU**s" who have gained spiritual understanding and insight from within the pages of this book.

To perceive the full message that is contained within, it must be prayerfully read, and then re-read again and again, until we discover with amazement, and with a thankful heart, that the experiences of the Bride, as recorded within this book, are being relived within our life experience.

As we develop into this closer communion with Him as His Bride, He will begin to share with us His burden for mankind. Then, in union with Him, we together can progress into all that He intends in the ages that are before us.

Here, He will reveal the fullness of His love to us, without end.

Books by Wade E. Taylor

The Secret of the Stairs

Waterspouts of Glory

Books: $9.99 plus $2.00
shipping & handling
(NY residents add 8% tax)
Order 10 or more and receive 20% discount.

The following are available on a free-will offering basis:

Pinecrest Bible Training Center Catalog and School information

<u>The Banner</u>

A quarterly publication promoting spiritual growth
and maturity. (Suggested donation $10 per year.)

Back issues of The Banner also available

The Christian Maturity Series

A series of tracts by Wade E. Taylor
promoting spiritual growth and maturity.

Please write:

PINECREST BIBLE BOOKSTORE
P.O. Box 320
Salisbury Center, NY 13454-0320